CW00549920

*Sylvia Sweeting
with best wishes
from*

Ronnie Coulbrough

The author describes his
experiences in
Southern Burma and
Rangoon Jail from
January 1942 to April 1945.

MEMORIES

OF A

PERPETUAL
SECOND LIEUTENANT

BY

C.R.L. COUBROUGH

First Published in Great Britian
by
WILTON 65
Flat Top House, Bishop Wilton, York. YO42 1RY
1999

ISBN 0 947828 75 3

To June and to my daughter and son-in-law, Pauline and Simon de Galleani, my son and daughter-in-law, David and Victoria Coubrough, my grandchildren, Eleanor, Isabel, Imogen and Rosalind de Galleani; Olivia, Alice, Emily and Jonathan Coubrough and any of their descendants who may be interested in an ancestor's story.

CONTENTS

PART lll

LIBERATION

APPENDICES

ILLUSTRATIONS

LIST OF MAPS

PROLOGUE

The Captain of a Swiss Air Boeing 707 from Zurich to Hong Kong one February morning in the early seventies announced that we were approaching the coast of Burma. After a week's skiing in Davos I was en route (with stopovers in Hong Kong and Bangkok) to join June at her brother's house in Sydney - and thence to Fiji.

I looked down to see nothing but cloud or early morning mist. Suddenly a gap appeared and there, thousands of feet below, jutting out starkly dark into the shimmering sunlit waters of the River Salween, I recognised the Martaban Peninsular. I saw the road at sea level encompassing the hilly point. I remembered rounding a corner into full view across the river of the city of Moulmein, just captured by the Japanese, and seeing a shell explode on the ground uncomfortably close to our truck. This was the first occasion when I had been under enemy fire - unless one counts that evening in the autumn of 1940 when three German bombs had fallen on Hadley Wood Golf Course some 200 yards from our home, where my parents and I were reading books after dinner - (no TV in those days).

The gap widened. I could see further up the Salween - one of the great rivers of Southern Asia, magnificent but to me sometimes sinister - which played such an important role in my life some thirty years earlier. The gap did not extend far enough to enable me to see Pa-an, the small township some 25 miles up river on the East bank. It was on the other side of the river opposite Pa-an that my Battalion, positioned some 15 miles from our nearest supporting troops, had been defeated and finally overrun in the 'Battle of Pa-an' in the early hours of the morning of the 12th February 1942.

In fact the gap then closed - perhaps symbolically - before

1

I could see Moulmein and identify the jail where I had spent the first three months of over three years as a prisoner of the Japanese.

I sat back in my comfortable seat and reflected on those stirring times when I was a 20 year old recently commissioned Second Lieutenant in the 7th Battalion of the 10th Baluch Regiment. Some words from an autobiographical poem (Cricket Master) by John Betjeman flashed through my mind:

> *I am thirty summers older,*
> *richer, wickeder and colder,*
> *fuller too of care........*

Hopefully the word 'wickeder' was inappropriate. Unfortunately the rest, particularly the last four words, were apposite. (How much more so now when I am over 50 summers older). I remembered the excitement, the comradeship and the unselfishness of those days. But I also remembered how it had all changed after the battle of Pa-an, some of it gradually over the ensuing months, but all of it utterly and for ever.

It was unusual for me at that time to reflect on the past. I was far too busy. But that flight over the Martaban Peninsular, however brief, brought back so many memories that it gave me the idea for the first time that when I was less busy I should put some of my wartime experiences down on paper.

INTRODUCTION

It was in 1976 after a visit to Burma on a cultural tour, that I first put pen to paper. I wrote an account entitled 'Burma Revisited.' An edited version of this is included in Appendix E.

But it was not until June 1987, recuperating after an operation in the beautiful tranquil surroundings of Le Cap Estel, a small hotel near Eze-sur-Mere in the South of France, that I started to write an account of my wartime memories. For a long time I did this sporadically - always when we have visited Le Cap Estel, which for many years we did annually. Sitting on the terrace gazing out over the Mediterranean Sea, there could not have been a greater contrast to the events I was describing.

In July 1996 I completed the first part of my Wartime Memories. This described my experiences as a recently commissioned Second Lieutenant, just 20 years old, in a newly formed battalion of the Indian Army, trained for desert warfare against the Germans but flung into the Burmese jungle to fight the Japanese. It covered the period from my battalion's landing in Burma on 16th January 1942 until my comrades and I arrived in Rangoon by sea from Moulmein on 26th June of that year as prisoners of the Japanese. It described my part in the Battle of Pa-an (pronounced Pa-arn), my capture and the early months of captivity. I circulated copies among family and friends who were interested.

It was not until January 1999 that I completed the second part of my Memories. This described my time in Rangoon Jail, the march out of the Jail of the so-called fit prisoners on 25th April 1945 and our rescue by my old Division, of which my Battalion was still part, four days later. It described my first few weeks of freedom culminating in my arrival home on 24th June 1945. It also contained my final reflections on my experiences during those

3

eventful years.

During the time between completing the two parts, I carried out a considerable amount of research. Some of this was into the Battle of Pa-an, including reading Japanese accounts - not always accurate I have to say. As a result of this research I made some alterations to my general account of the Battle but not to the description of my personal experiences. These alterations were circulated with copies of Part II. In fact I had originally intended to confine my description of the Battle to that contained in the text of a speech (Appendix F) which at the invitation of John Randle, at that time a retired Brigadier and President of the Baluch Officers' Dinner Club. I had made at a dinner in London on 12th February 1992 to mark the fiftieth anniversary of the Battle of Pa-an. But my account is now a full one. It not only describes my own experiences during the Battle but includes my considered thoughts on its course. It is as accurate as I can make it.

I have included in Appendix D with the permission of John Randle, his description of an extraordinary episode which took place in Pa-an in November 1945, three months or so after the Japanese surrender. The reader will understand why he entitled this 'Full Circle' and why I wanted to include it.

In this final version of my Memories I have combined both Parts. I have edited what I have previously written. I have taken on board some views expressed and information given in correspondence. As a result I have embellished some anecdotes and have made minor alterations to the text. I have too made further additions to my story, in particular expanding Chapter VIII which describes my time in Moulmein Jail.

I have described my feelings towards the Japanese and my opinion of them during my captivity. These have changed over the years since the War, and in 1996 I was happy to join the Burma Campaign Fellowship Group whose raison d'être is to encourage reconciliation between those who fought each other in Burma in

4

the Second World War. Nowadays I refer to the Japanese as 'Japanese' and not as 'Japs' or 'Nips,' as indeed I have done in this chapter and elsewhere when reflecting on events. I considered doing the same throughout my Memories. I decided against this as my Memories, so much of which comprise a narrative of events at the time, must reflect my thoughts at that time. When we were in action against the Japanese, everyone without exception referred to them as 'Japs.' My imprisonment was a time when the Japanese despised us for having allowed ourselves to be taken prisoners and it was one when we gained satisfaction by referring to them contemptuously as 'Japs' or 'Nips.'

I have described what I have written as *The Memories of a Perpetual Second Lieutenant*. When I was taken prisoner there was no automatic promotion to Lieutenant after six months. Although all the Second Lieutenant POWs were promoted in India, we did not know this in Rangoon Jail for a long time. In any event the Japanese continued to treat us as Second Lieutenants.

These reminiscences are frankly autobiographical and subjective, more so perhaps than some would like. They are primarily for my family and friends. At the suggestion of others, I have on occasions analysed my feelings at the time. I can remember some of the events and verbal exchanges with absolute clarity. But with the passage of time, other parts of my experiences have receded into a grey background. It is, however, surprising how much did come back to me when I thought about the events, studied maps and read the accounts of others. I have done my best to give a completely truthful account throughout, whether I conducted myself creditably or perhaps not quite as well as I would have wished. In this connection one or two of my readers have suggested that I have been rather hard on myself at times. I have considered those particular episodes, but have not altered my account of any of them. Sometimes, however, I have added an explanatory comment.

I felt that I had a story to tell. I have told it as accurately and as honestly as I could. I have also tried to make it readable and on occasions, when the circumstances allowed, amusing.

Notes

(1)   The battle, in which I took part, was fought on ground to the north of the village of Kuzeik on the west bank of the River Salween opposite Pa-an on the east bank, from where the Japanese attack was mounted, albeit indirectly. It is known to the survivors of the Battle and is referred to in the history of the 10th Baluch Regiment as the 'Battle of Pa-an.'

(2)   The books which contain accounts of the Battle of Pa-an include *Eastern Epic* by Compton Mackenzie, *The Longest Retreat* (a masterpiece of inventive journalism and a tribute to the colourful imagination of the author) by Tim Carew, *Dawns Like Thunder; the Retreat from Burma* by Alfred Draper to whom I told part of my story and finally and authoritatively *BURMA 1942: The Japanese Invasion* by Major-General Ian Lyall Grant in collaboration with Dr Kazuo Tamayama (published in January 1999 by the Zampi Press of Chichester, West Sussex).

PART I

ON ACTIVE SERVICE

We are they who come faster than fate: we are
         they who ride early or late:
We storm at your ivory gate.
         Pale kings of the sunset, beware!'

The War Song of the Saracans   James Elroy Flecker

MAP 1

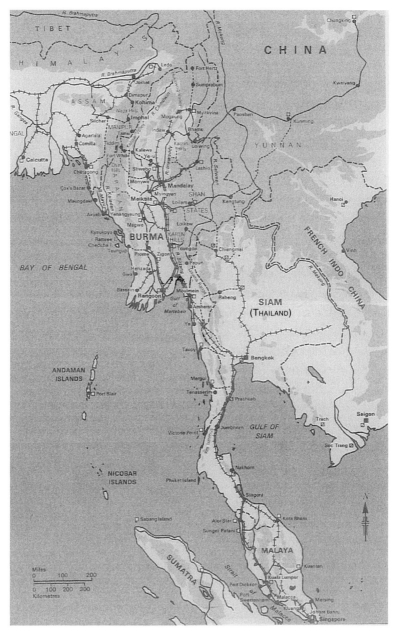

<small>BURMA AND SURROUNDING COUNTRIES 1942</small>

CHAPTER I

THE FIRST THREE WEEKS

The 7th Battalion of the 10th Baluch Regiment (7 Baluch) landed in Rangoon on the 16th January 1942.

I had joined the battalion when it was stationed in Madras in September 1941. I had been commissioned as a Second Lieutenant after a 6 month course at the Cadet College in Bangalore in Southern India. Shortly after joining the battalion I had left for a signals course in Poona and was away for many weeks.

7 Baluch had soon joined the newly formed 17th Indian Division under the command of Major General Jackie Smyth V.C.[1] This was trained on the plains of Central India (Ahmednagar and Kedgaon) for service in the Middle East. Despite the entry of Japan into the war on the 8th December 1941 and their early successes in Malaya, the Division had continued to train for desert warfare against the Germans. Two of the brigades (44 and 45) had sailed for the Middle East in late December and early January 1942. They had however been diverted in mid-ocean to Singapore. Fortunately our 46 Brigade and 17th Indian Division Head Quarters were sent to Calcutta for embarkation to Burma.

After disembarking, we spent a couple of days training in some jungle near Rangoon. It could not have been a bigger contrast to the terrain over which we had been trained. As Signals Officer, I discovered that the new wireless sets which had worked so admirably in India were useless amongst the trees. Also our heliographs were not required!

By then the Japanese were commencing their invasion of Burma. On the 20th January they defeated the 16th Indian Brigade at Kawkereik on the Burmese/Thai frontier, east of Moulmein to where our forces retired.

We were moved south. For the next three weeks we were continually moved around. For most of the time we were in the front line in as much as there were none of our troops between us and the Japanese - wherever they might be. There was however the great barrier of the River Salween.

In addition to carrying out my duties as Signals Officer, I was on occasions employed in taking out patrols.

I remember particularly two episodes during these weeks.

1. The Flotilla on the River Donthami.

On a day late in January, Battalion HQ was at Thaton. This was the largest town in Southern Burma apart from Rangoon and Moulmein. It was also the district HQ for the civil administration. Moulmein, which was to fall on 31st January had not yet been attacked. Our C company commanded by Siri (Captain S.K. Korla) was positioned across the Salween at Pa-an. This was at the end of the only other road from Thailand to the Salween in Southern Burma. At Pa-an there was a ferry, from which the road ran to Duyinzeik, where there was another ferry and then the road to Thaton.

No-one knew whether there were any Japs in the area. Siri had not had any contact with any.

We had commandeered a large pleasure boat and a small fast motor boat. The CO sent for Bill Greenwood, another Second Lieutenant who was Company Officer to Second Lieutenant John Randle the B Company Commander, and me. He told us what he wanted. One of us was to take the motor boat with two or three men down the Donthami to its confluence with the Salween and to cruise around there to see if there was any sign of the Japs. The other was to take the pleasure boat, with a number of well-armed men down the Donthami and then up the Salween to Pa-an, where it could be of use to C Company. He left it to us to decide who should take which boat.

Bill Greenwood and I had a cheerful argument as to which of us was the senior and hence Commodore of the 7 Baluch Flotilla. But there was no dispute about the choice of boats. Bill wanted to drive the speedboat. I wanted the adventure of taking the pleasure boat up the Salween to Pa-an.

The CO introduced me to two brothers, middle-aged civilians, who were in Thaton. I believe their name was Finlay and that they were rubber planters somewhere in Southern Burma. Certainly they knew the area and the River Salween well. We pored over my map. I questioned them about the nature of the terrain on the east bank of the Salween and whether it would be easily accessible to the Japs. In view of what happened next day, their replies were irrelevant. But it did mean that I studied the map of that part of the Salween, down which I was to travel as a prisoner some two weeks later. In fact the only comments of theirs I can remember were their expressions of pleasure that I appreciated the beauty of the scenery in their beloved Southern Burma, despite my reasons for being there.

The next morning with a number of men under an NCO provided by John Randle from B Company armed with automatic weapons and the Motor Transport Havildar from HQ Company, I took over the pleasure boat together with a Burmese boatman at Duyinzeik. Sandbags were filled up, placed and piled up quite high with gaps for our weapons under the direction of the NCO along the starboard side of the boat. Satisfied on inspection, I personally took the wheel of the boat and feeling pleasurably excited pushed the lever to 'full steam ahead.' We moved off, gained speed but after some 20 yards or so the engine just stopped. We drifted into the bank where we spent the next few hours. The MT Havildar and the Burmese boatman were quite unable to repair the engine. I was no help as the internal combustion engine (or indeed any engine) was and still is a complete mystery to me.

My mood of intense frustration and disappointment was not improved to see a Brigadier striding towards me along the bank from the ferry. This was Brigadier J.K. Jones the commander of the 16th Indian Brigade, fresh from defeat at Kawkereik. 7 Baluch was attached to his brigade at the time. The following exchanges took place:

Brigadier Jones (without the trace of a smile)

"What has happened here?"

Second Lieutenant Coubrough explained what he had intended to do and that he had been frustrated by engine failure which so far had not been remedied.

Brigadier Jones (impatiently)

"It is your command."

Second Lieutenant Coubrough (not a great respecter of rank in those days)

"I am a Signals Officer not a motor mechanic, Sir."

He gave me an old-fashioned look but moved off without further comment.

Even my friend John Randle, was critical.

"I give you some of my best men and you leave them strewn all over the Burmese countryside!"

I certainly did not stand for that! But it had been a bitterly disappointing day.

The other boat in the 7 Baluch Flotilla had started from Kyettuywethaung, a little way down the Donthami, where Bill Greenwood was stationed with a detachment of B Company. He had a fast uneventful trip in the motor boat to the confluence with the Salween, cruised around and then returned. He did not see any Japs.

2. Attempted crossing of the River Salween that never was.

After the fall of Moulmein, our Brigade took up a position along the west bank of the Salween northwards from Martaban.

There were gaps between units which were extensively patrolled. I was in command of one such patrol one night when suddenly all hell was let loose. The west bank of the Salween erupted with firing. I was at the time near the river and immediately lined my men up along the bank. I watched the firework display for a number of minutes. I had very keen eyesight in those days and the river was lit up. Whatever had initially 'triggered off' the firing, I was absolutely sure that there were no boats attempting to cross the Salween near my position. I accordingly continued my patrol of the segment allotted to me and reported back to the Adjutant before going off to sleep. Next day there were no reports of any landings. I put it down to an example of windy firing, which I learned subsequently was to be quite a common occurrence during the retreat to India, as it was in the Malayan/Singapore campaign.

However, that evening in the officers' mess at Battalion HQ, when we switched on the news from London as usual, the very first item was as follows:

"Last night the Japanese attempted to cross the River Salween in force. They were repulsed with heavy losses. Barge loads of the enemy were wiped out."

Up until that time, I had always believed in the accuracy of the news given out by our side, whether it was the number of German aircraft shot down in a day by the RAF in the Battle of Britain or whatever. But never again.

MAP 2

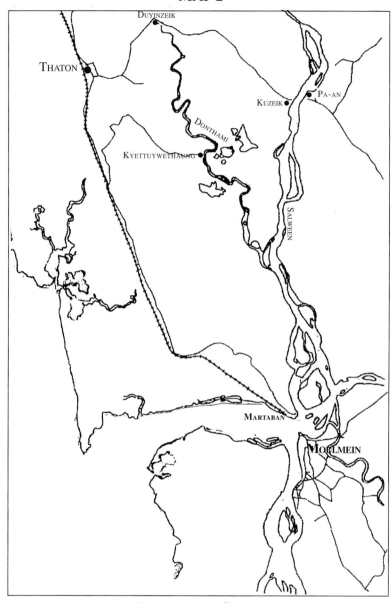

AREA OF SOUTH BURMA
RELEVANT TO CHAPTERS I TO VIII

CHAPTER II

PRELUDE TO THE BATTLE

The 'phoney war' for me ended in the morning of the 9th February. I had thoroughly enjoyed the last few weeks. The weather had been perfect, not too hot with cloudless skies - (a complete contrast to that often experienced by 7 Baluch on subsequent occasions (e.g. the Battle of Imphal) and to that so often shown on TV programmes of the fighting in Burma). The scenery was idyllic. Although we had been in the front-line we had never actually encountered any Japs, whom I for one grossly under estimated. There was, however, always the exciting prospect of running into some at any time. Nevertheless, the fact remains that the only time when we had been under fire was when the Battalion had run the gauntlet of shell fire from Moulmein as we rounded the point of the Martaban Peninsular to take up our position on the west bank of the Salween.

That morning, I was walking over a sparsely-vegetated hill with the Second-in-Command, Major Pat Dunn (an Anglo-Indian who became a Lieutenant-General in the Indian Army after independence). 7 Baluch had taken over from 1/7 Gurkhas their position on the west bank of the Salween opposite Pa-an. I suddenly heard the sound of planes. Then I saw the first two flying straight towards us low over the jungle. Fortunately there was a nearby slit trench dug by the Gurkhas. We threw ourselves into it. The air attack was long and prolonged. Waves of Jap planes were flown from Chieng Mai in Thailand. They dived down with ear-splitting screeches, flattened out at a low level and peppered us with anti-personnel bombs. Pat Dunn and I were in the centre of the target area. Every now and then we were showered with earth.

Fortunately, however, we escaped a direct hit.

Immediately the bombing stopped, I climbed out of the trench in order to deal with casualties. There were none in the immediate vicinity; but I met a number of leaderless men from one of the rifle companies, unsettled by the bombing, coming up the hill. They told me the Japs were attacking. I took over command, steadied the men and placed them in defensive positions just below the brow of the hill facing downwards with a field of fire over the relatively clear area. Although there was a lot of noise, I did not personally believe this was a Jap attack. Nevertheless, it was always possible that they had crossed the river either to the south or north under cover of darkness; and had advanced unseen through the jungle. If this had been so, the bombing could have been the prelude to an attack. I made it absolutely clear to every single man that no one was to fire without my order. This was just as well as out of the jungle at the foot of the hill into the field of fire there appeared not the Japs but the CO and the Subedar Major!

"Just what the hell do you think you are doing Coubrough?"

The Colonel asked me this question in a tone of voice in which he contrived to combine amazement with accusation.

I suppose it is possible for someone to have been so deflated as I was; but it is difficult to see how. For the first time in my life, men had responded to my leadership. I was confident that if the Japs should attack we would give a good account of ourselves and hit back at them after having passively endured the bombing over the last few hours. Then the adrenalin, which had been coursing through my veins, swiftly ebbed away, as I explained my actions to a Commanding Officer who listened in total silence.

[When writing this account I remembered the previous most embarrassing episode in my young life. The Scouts were giving a jamboree in the gym at my prep school in front of the two senior headmasters and the staff as well as the rest of the school. We had erected a tall pole with a tin effigy of our

Founder, Lord Baden-Powell, stuck to the top. I was responsible for its erection. Suddenly, to my horror, I saw the pole starting to sway. Sure enough the 'silly thing' crashed down in front of all, decapitating our 'Great Founder'! There was a stunned silence. It had been the great day of our Scout Leader, who was the junior of three headmasters. The silence was broken as he spat the following words at me in an uncontrolled rage:

"Coubrough, as a Patrol Leader you are as much use to me as a sick headache."

The last two words came out in a crescendo of sound].

Actually, of course, the episodes were not comparable. In fact, that evening in the Officers' Mess at Battalion Headquarters, in front of all the officers other than those out with their companies on the perimeter, the CO called for silence. To my intense surprise, he then went on to praise my conduct during the episode and to say how pleased he was with me. My initial reaction was one of embarrassment; but there are few who object to basking in the approval of a strong personality. Moreover, I have to confess that I rather enjoyed being the CO's 'blue-eyed boy' for the very first time.

What did give me real pleasure, however, was the complete change in attitude towards me of Subedar-Major Kirpa Ram. He was an absolutely first rate professional soldier of fine physique. In fact he was everything that I was not. I was not the only junior officer who was a little in awe of him. After the bombing episode, he treated me with a respect which at times had seemed rather lacking before. Unfortunately I had only two days left to savour this new relationship. I would like to believe that if fate (or rather the Japanese army) had decreed otherwise, it would have continued to flourish.

There were further air raids the next morning and on the following day, 11th February. I was not in the target area on either occasion. The three air raids did cause a certain amount of physical damage and considerable disruption to, amongst others, the signalling arrangements, where there was a shortage of equipment in any event. But the casualties were in fact a great deal less than might have been expected considering the weight and length of the air attacks. On the 9th February there were three killed and thirty wounded. These did, however, include the whole of the Intelligence Section, (part of the Headquarters Company), except for the Jemadar in command, who was badly shaken. They were all together in one place. I had had quite a bit of contact with them since our arrival in Burma, and knew the Jemadar well. It was brought home to me for the first time that there was another side to the war which I had been enjoying as an exciting adventure.

CHAPTER III

THE BATTLE OF PA-AN

The Brigade Plan

We had not been in our position opposite Pa-an long before Second Lieutenant Pettigrew, our liaison officer with Brigade HQ was driven up in a 15 cwt truck with our orders from Brigade. [John Randle, Pettigrew and I had been posted to 7 Baluch on the same day in September 1941 on passing out at Bangalore Cadet College. Whereas neither of us had met John Randle, Pettigrew and I had been in the same platoon since joining up at Aldershot in December 1940. We heartily disliked each other].

I was present when he handed Brigade's orders to the CO When he moved away to read them, Pettigrew characteristically held forth to the rest of us:

"It is a brilliant plan, absolutely brilliant. You are to stay here and fight to the last man and the last round - until the Dogras counter-attack the Japs from the rear."

He then added - "Sorry chaps, I must be off. I am needed at Brigade."

With that the truck drove off at speed. [In repeating this little episode, which I did frequently in Moulmein Jail - and with embellishments such as "Pettigrew had one foot in the truck as he told us how lucky we were to be part of such a brilliant plan," I was not being fair to Dan Pettigrew. He was not the least bit concerned about his lonely 15 mile drive back to Duyinzeik. He merely wanted to impress on us how important he was].

There was, of course, more to the Brigade plan than Pettigrew's dramatic summary! John Randle in his account sets it

19

out in professional terms:

"The battalion's task was to deny the ferry crossing to the Japs in Pa-an and by establishing patrol bases north and south of its position near the village of Kuzeik, to identify and delay expected enemy crossings, until the Brigade Reserve Battalion 5th/17th Dogras (The Dogras) could counter-attack and drive them into the river."

Events during the night of the 10th/11th February and daylight hours on the 11th February.

On the night of the 10th/11th February, a patrol base near Pagat four miles to the south, comprising a platoon each from A and B Companies was wiped out; and B Company, less that platoon on its way to a routine relief of the base, was attacked and only extricated itself after some brisk exchanges. Under cover of darkness, the river had been crossed by 215 Regiment, comprising three Battalions of the formidable Japanese 33rd Division, which after years of fighting in China had been trained for jungle warfare. They were known throughout the Japanese Army as 'The White Tigers'.

On the morning of the 11th February, Brigade was informed that the Japs had crossed the Salween in force and that an attack was expected. There was no further communication that afternoon. The two signallers, sent to us by Brigade, were unable to make contact on their wireless.

As mentioned above, there was an air raid during the day. This went on well into the afternoon. As soon as it was over the Indian Gunners ran away. They comprised a section of a mountain battery with 3.7 Howitzer mountain guns. They had been positioned by Brigade for the purpose of shelling Pa-an across the river. They were not under Colonel Dyer's command. They abandoned their guns and ran off into the jungle crying out to each other in Urdu -

MAP 3

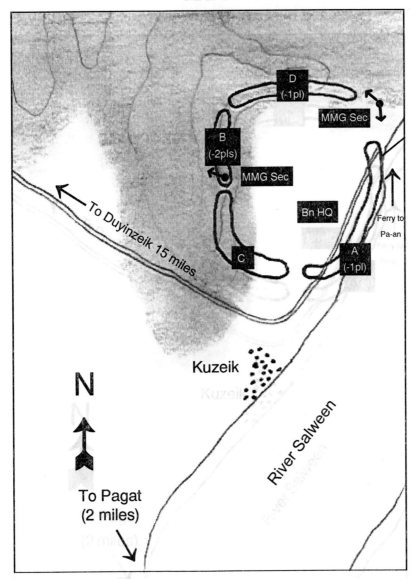

THE DISPOSITIONS OF 7 BALUCH
AT NIGHTFALL ON FEBRUARY 11TH

'Run, run'. They were pursued by their British Officer, shouting "Come back, you ....s, come back." No one came back.

The situation as darkness fell on the 11th February

That evening we had supper early in the officers' mess at Battalion Headquarters. As usual we did ourselves pretty well - (apart from never drinking any alcohol). We were joined by two or three of the officers from the Companies on the perimeter. Despite the comradeship, it was eerie sitting there eating when we knew that we were surrounded by Japanese troops lurking in the jungle waiting to attack. However, this had no effect on my healthy appetite. In fact, if I had known that it was to be another seventy-five hours before I had my next meal, I would have eaten even more.

The road to Duyinzeik commenced at the ferry terminus opposite Pa-an. It ran along parallel to the river Salween (about eight hundred yards wide at that point) to the village of Kuzeik where it turned at right angles straight north-west for fifteen miles to the ferry crossing on the River Donthami (about one hundred yards wide at that point) at Duyinzeik. That evening the battalion was deployed in a perimeter facing south, west and north with the river to the east at the back. A Company HQ and two Platoons (Captain Bill Cayley) was situated at the rear between the river and that segment of the road, running between the ferry terminus and Kuzeik. In addition to watching the river in case there was an attempted crossing from Pa-an, the Company faced south to cover any attack along the road from Kuzeik. The other three Companies were deployed on the lip of a saucer-like position, with its back to the river - from left to right - C Company HQ and three platoons (Captain Siri Kanth Korla); B Company HQ and one platoon (one platoon having been wiped out as mentioned above and another sent out on patrol) (Second Lieutenant John Randle) and facing

22

North West and North D coy HQ and three platoons (Second Lieutenant 'Jake' Jervis). Battalion HQ and all HQ Company troops, not otherwise deployed, were at the rear to the west of the section of the road from the ferry terminus to Kuzeik. The MMG platoon had machine guns deployed across the battalion front. (These dispositions are depicted in Map 3). As the slopes of the saucer were steep and thickly jungled, there was no depth to the position. As a result the Battalion's mortars could not, even at minimum range, provide any close defensive fire. The same would have applied to the 3.7 Howitzer mountain guns, even if the Indian Gunners had not run away. The Companies were spread out thinly along the perimeter with large gaps between them. Both the disruption caused by the air raids and the heavy patrolling programme had made it difficult for the battalion to develop the defensive position beyond slit trenches. Moreover, there was no wire or other defensive stores.

The course of the Battle

The Japanese assault began at 2.00am in the morning of the 12th February.

The attack came from the south west with two Japanese Battalions on C Company and the depleted B Company. There was no prior fire support. The moon had risen. The first indication our forward troops had of the attack was when they saw the moonlight glinting on those awesome long Japanese bayonets, as the attackers moved out silently from the cover of the jungle. They then attacked in wave after wave with fixed bayonets and drawn swords - shouting and screaming at the top of their voices.

For over four hours, although greatly outnumbered, the Baluchis stood their ground against an enemy who displayed fanatical courage and accepted heavy casualties. Siri led a number of counter attacks before C Company was finally overrun. In my speech on

23

the fiftieth anniversary of the battle (Appendix F) I referred to his receiving the DSO, but I omitted to mention that it was an immediate award. The depleted B Company held out a little longer until the Japs infiltrated behind and overran it.

There was then a pause while the Japs regrouped. They put in their final assault in daylight on the rest of the Battalion. There were instances of spirited resistance. There were fine performances. But in all honesty the battle was lost once the positions of C Company and the depleted B Company were overrun and the perimeter breached. The promised counter-attack from the Dogras never materialised.

My experiences during the Battle

I was lying asleep at Battalion HQ under a blanket, fully clothed with boots on of course, when the attack began. Firing erupted all round the perimeter. I heard the Colonel call out to the Adjutant (Captain Hugh Mercer) "The river front Hugh." They then crossed the road and joined Bill Cayley in A Company HQ. Unfortunately they were compelled to remain there until dawn, pinned down by 'friendly fire,' from a section of the MMG platoon deployed nearby.

Major Dunn, the second-in-command, ordered me to stay with the two Brigade Signallers to make sure that they remained at their post and did everything possible to make contact either with Brigade HQ or the Dogras. I did this for a time; but then decided to delegate the task to a reliable NCO. I felt that I could be of more use elsewhere. I returned regularly; but it was quite obvious that they would never make contact. They had been trying unsuccessfully all afternoon. This was the only order I received during the battle.

For hour after hour, we listened to the fusillade of shots varied by the shouts and screams of the Japs, as they made bayonet charges, and the responding war cries of our men. Would the Dogras never come?

I remember meeting the Subedar-Major and commenting to him on how well I thought C Company must be fighting. His craggy dark features split open and were illuminated by a large smile as he agreed with me. [He was a Dogra, as were the men of C Company, although this in no way affected his loyalty to the Punjabi Mussulmen and Pathans in the Battalion].[2]

I also remember deciding on my own initiative to take my orderly and to try to get through to B Company HQ. We were still some way short when bullets started 'plopping' into the undergrowth. We pressed on for a little, but the number of bullets increased. My orderly looked at me in a questioning and rather unhappy manner. I decided that it was not such a good idea after all. I had no information about the whereabouts of the Dogras or orders to pass on to John Randle. Moreover, while I had informed my Havildar (sergeant) of my intentions, I had not cleared them with Major Dunn, partly because I was disobeying his orders to stay with the Brigade Signallers. My orderly and I went back to Battalion HQ.

There was another British Officer attached to the Headquarters Company, Second Lieutenant George Holden. He was senior to me and in addition to his specialised duties he commanded HQ Company when the occasion required (e.g. on a march). In the absence of any orders he had organised a strong point. "We are strong here" he pointed out to me, as he strode confidently around, carrying the Thompson sub-machine gun, of which, alone among the officers, he was the fortunate possessor. [He made full use of this a few hours later. A Jap platoon formed up outside the thicket in which he was hiding. Holden stepped out and mowed them down, emptying a whole drum, before running off through the jungle to the road to Duyinzeik]. I decided that I would ask Major Dunn's permission, if there were no other duties for me, to take some of my signallers and reinforce Holden's strong point. It was now daylight and for some time there had been an ominous silence from the direction of C and B Companies. I hurried back to Battalion HQ. There I met Toots (Captain Bruce Toothill, the Quarter-Master), who told me that the CO and the Adjutant had returned and that the CO had just left, crossing the road again towards the river.

I ran across the road on to the foot of a hill, bare of all vegetation. I saw a number of riflemen and in the middle of them the Colonel and Major Dunn, all walking, spread out and not in any order, across the hill in the direction of Kuzeik. I moved quickly towards the Colonel. Mortar shells started to fall on the hill, fired from Pa-an, in full view across the river. We all, except for one, began to run for cover. I called out slowly in Urdu, in what was intended to be a cheery, reassuring tone of voice: "As quickly as possible." The Colonel who continued his unhurried walk, spoke in English in a loud voice: "There is no hurry." They were to be his last words. I ran up and fell into step beside him. Side by side we walked - oh so slowly - across that exploding hill and down towards the cover of the jungle below, when we were thrust aside. Someone ran between us and rushed down into the jungle. Perhaps he had a point to make.

With the Colonel leading but not giving any orders, a number of us proceeded through difficult terrain toward Kuzeik. After he had climbed down the side of a deep ravine, Jerry Dyer turned right and followed it up to the road. He climbed up on to the road. He then set off at a cracking pace, grasping his walking stick halfway up the handle. As I was climbing up the side of the ravine, preparatory to stepping on to the road, something made me stop. I studied the road ahead and the terrain on either side intently. Not far ahead the road disappeared to the right (towards Duyinzeik) round a high rock. There was thick jungle all the way along on the left, largely below the road. On the right-hand side the road skirted

26

a steep hill and there was no cover at all except for a small flat area on which a clump of high grass was growing. This was in front of the high rock to which I have referred. I suddenly saw the tall grass move. There was not a breath of wind. I shouted:

"Look out Sir. Take cover. Japs ahead."

The Colonel took no notice but walked on at the same pace. Three shots rang out. The first hit him in the right wrist, which he clutched dropping his walking stick. The next two knocked him to the ground where he lay still on the road.

I realised there was no point in climbing on to the road and running to help him. The place from where the shots were fired was out of pistol range. In any event I lacked the upper body strength to lift him. On the other hand I had pinpointed the exact location of the Jap position. There was room for only two or three at the most. I needed fire power to knock it out and men to help me carry the Colonel back. I had not seen any of the riflemen accompanying us carrying an automatic weapon; but I had noticed a rifle with a grenade cup. I decided to try to get hold of this rifleman as well as one or two others. These thoughts were running through my mind as I turned round and looked back down the ravine. There was no one in sight. I climbed down and called out; but no one answered. All had gone to ground. Before setting off in search of help, I decided to check the situation on the road. I climbed half way up the side to look over the top and saw to my surprise that Jerry Dyer had managed to stand up. He was staggering back towards me. I climbed up on to the road as fast as I could and ran to help him. I supported him back along the road. When we reached the top of the ravine, I was immensely cheered to find that two Jawans (young Indian soldiers) were down below ready to help. One of them climbed half way up the side of the ravine, while the other remained at the bottom. Between the three of us we lowered Jerry Dyer down into the temporary safety of the ravine.

This all took quite a bit of time during which we were 'sitting targets.' But not a shot was fired. This made me conclude that there was only one Jap in that clump of high grass in front of the rock. He probably had orders to fire at anyone who came along the road and was conserving his ammunition. I do not believe that his failure to shoot us in the back was an act of chivalry. That was not a characteristic of the Japanese.

I went ahead down the ravine and selected a grassy spot near the river but out of sight from the other bank. It was as comfortable as I could find. It also gave him a reasonable chance of avoiding detection, until the Dogras arrival of which I had not given up hope. The two riflemen carried the Colonel down the ravine and laid him down as I directed. They then disappeared while I was dressing the Colonel's wounds. I did this, as best I could, using both our field dressings.

We were alone in the ravine for at least an hour, perhaps longer, before the Japs started to search the area. I did not stay with Jerry Dyer all the time, but went up and down the ravine, climbing the sides and poking my head out to see what was happening or if I could find any of our men to organise. I saw no-one. I always returned to Jerry Dyer and stayed with him for a while. On these occasions, before he lapsed into a coma, he would gesture with his hands that I should leave him. He was unable to speak because his jaw had been shattered by a bullet. I had no intention of leaving him until the last possible minute. Equally I saw no point in dying beside him in an exchange of fire with the Japs; and I certainly had no intention, either then or indeed at any time, of giving myself up. I considered it my duty to do my best to find my way back to our forces. I know that Jerry Dyer agreed.

I had selected an excellent hiding place in a bush growing high up out of the side of the ravine. As soon as the Japs started searching the bushes near the ravine, I climbed up into my hiding place. I heard a lot of jabbering when they found Jerry Dyer. I was told afterwards that they had killed him. But I could not be sure at the time as there were sporadic single shots coming from all directions including that one. They may well have taken him by stretcher along the firm ground beside the river up to the ferry and decided to kill him there. Certainly when I went past the spot at dusk, I was vastly relieved to find that there was no corpse left for the vultures.

The Japs searched the ravine thoroughly - usually in pairs. More than once a Jap stopped, looked at my hiding place and then moved on. But on one occasion the second of two Japs, both armed with rifles going up the ravine from the river, having looked up and moved on, suddenly reappeared and stood below, staring up in my direction. I crouched, absolutely motionless, balanced on the balls of my feet, with my pistol aimed at his face and my finger on the trigger. I realised that I had only one chance. Once I was sure that he had seen me, I had to kill him with my first shot, leap out of the bush and hurtle down the side of the ravine on to level ground without losing my balance. I then had to swing right to shoot the first Jap before he could use his rifle on me - one way or another. I planned to run like hell the short distance down the ravine to the river, engaging any more Japs coming up with my pistol. I had checked that there was firm ground between the water and the river bank. Running along this, I would have been in full view from the other side of the river, but any Jap seeing me would have been too far away to influence events. I would have been out of sight of the Japs searching my area and would hope to enter the jungle further down river.

For what seemed like several minutes I studied the face of the first Japanese I had ever properly seen. Then the second Jap moved on. He did not come back. There was no third Jap. In fact these two were the last Japs to search the ravine.

During my captivity I sometimes wondered how the second Jap could possibly have failed to see me, when he stared up at me for so long from such close range. We had been told that the Japs were myopic and could not see in the dark. Perhaps it was true. It was certainly dark in my hiding place. Fortunately they are a short race. But I did sometimes wonder whether he did in fact see not only me but my pistol trained on his face and he might not like to have admitted this to his comrade. The first explanation is more likely. Moreover I did remember at the time the necessity to remain absolutely still without moving a muscle. This was something I had learned as a boy when playing 'kick-the-tin,' (a variation of 'hide-and-seek'); by doing so I had more than once avoided detection despite being in full view of my seeker.

My considered thoughts on the Battle

Firstly, in regard to the later actions of the CO, I have to state at once that I joined him on the bare hill opposite Pa-an too late to learn his intentions. The Jap mortar fire did not exactly encourage conversation. I do not propose to speculate. All I will say is that no way would Jerry Dyer ever have raised his hands in surrender to the Japanese. Never would he have done that.

Despite its comprehensive defeat the Battalion has received much praise for its performance. I would only make two comments:

1.   In my opinion no infantry Company in the whole Burma Army would have put up a finer performance against overwhelming odds than that of C Company under the command of Captain Siri Kanth Korla.

2.   By repulsing all Japanese attacks and holding the perimeter intact for over four hours, we gave Brigade ample time to mount the counter-attack which was the centre-piece of their plan. 7 Baluch more than fulfilled its part. What in fact happened was that the Dogras were about half way along the road from Duyinzeik when they were ordered back by Brigade. They were given no reason for this decision. [I learnt this from their CO

30

Lieutenant Colonel Power in Moulmein Jail. He was taken prisoner by the Japs when the Sittang Bridge was blown up].

I will now quote from a letter which I wrote to Bruce Toothill (Toots) on the 17th November 1987, (when I was thanking him for information from his diary).

'Some years ago I found myself at the 17th Indian Division Reunion Dinner sitting within talking range of Guy Burton, then a retired Major General and a Director of an insurance company. You may remember that he was the Brigade Major, who many thought dominated Brigadier Roger Ekin. Colonel Power summed up the situation rather acidly in Moulmein: "I think we must say that, as a Brigadier, Major Burton was a failure!" I cross-examined him closely as to why we were left to our fate at Kuzeik (Pa-an) and why there was no counter-attack. He was a very unpopular man and everyone sitting near, including the other senior officers next to him at the top table, thoroughly enjoyed it. He was angry and embarrassed but quite unable to give any convincing answers.'

Whether the main responsibility lay with the Brigadier or the Brigade Major, one fact is incontrovertible. 7 Baluch were abandoned and left to be wiped out by the Japs. Five hundred and twenty-four officers, VCOs and men were killed (two hundred and eighty-nine) or taken prisoner (two hundred and thirty-five) by the Japs. Only five officers, three VCOs and sixty five men were able to fight their way out.

The Verdict of History

Major General Ian Lyall Grant and Dr Kazuo Tamayama have in *Burma 1942 - The Japanese Invasion*, written a book[3] which in the opinion of Field Marshal Lord Carver:

'...must henceforth be regarded as the most authoritative account' of the campaign in Burma in 1942.

There are eight pages on the Battle at Kuzeik (Pa-an).

They describe the end of the action as follows:

'Captain Siri Kanth Korla (who had been taken prisoner but escaped) was awarded an immediate DSO, a rare distinction. It had been a very desperate fight for a 'green' and unsupported battalion up against a much more powerful and experienced Japanese foe. The 7th/10th Baluch had fought it out with exemplary courage and this was not to be forgotten in 17 Division. There was, however, in British eyes at the time, a very ugly side to this action. The survivors were convinced that many of the wounded had been either shot or bayonetted to death, as indeed the figures seemed to indicate since few of the prisoners were wounded. The Japanese had learnt in China to fight a kill-or-be-killed war and this savage pattern, since the Japanese would never surrender, was increasingly to become the custom for both sides in the Burma war.'

In the final paragraph they write:

'The battle at Kuzeik was the first attempt by the British to stand their ground against a major Japanese attack, albeit in a hastily prepared position. Without wire or artillery support and against first-class opposition it was doomed to failure. Nevertheless it was a courageous and gallant effort and the lessons learned would not be forgotten.'

In fact it was not until over six months later that the Japanese were defeated for the first time in any battle on land against US, British or Commonwealth forces. This was in New Guinea by the Australians at Rabbi on 25th August 1942 and more significantly on the Kokoda Trail on 15th September 1942 when the Australians made a successful counter-attack. [While what I have written in this paragraph is generally accepted to be the truth, particularly by Australians, it is arguable that the first defeat suffered by the

Japanese on land was at Hlegu on 7th March 1942 when the 1st/ 4th Gurkhas cleared the road block and defeated a Japanese battalion. This action was however part of the Battle of Pegu which was not a defeat for the Japanese].

CHAPTER IV

ON THE RUN

The sounds of searching in the vicinity of my hiding place eventually died away. But I could hear continuous troop movement along the road.

I studied my map and took stock of my situation. The ravine came down from that segment of the road, which commencing at the ferry terminus opposite Pa-an ran along parallel to the river (about eight hundred yards wide at that point) to the village of Kuzeik where it turned at right angles. It then ran straight north-west to Duyinzeik where there was a ferry across the River Donthami (about one hundred yards wide at that point). The road then ran on to Thaton. Brigade headquarters were there.

For the time being I was trapped between the road in constant use by the Japs, the village of Kuzeik on one side and the ferry terminus opposite Pa-an on the other. I therefore had plenty of time to arrive at the decision which was the most important in my life to date. I considered all the options long and hard. I put myself in the place of the Jap commander. I thought I was such a 'clever Dick' - and I got it all wrong!

I decided to avoid the road to Duyinzeik. I reasoned as follows:

The Japs would decide to exploit their victory over us, which had given them the Pa-an crossing of the river Salween, by advancing quickly up the road to Duyinzeik and trying to seize the ferry crossing of the river Donthami. This would open up the only road from Pa-an to Thaton. They would surely need this to bring up their transport. As the Dogras had not counter-attacked the Japs as planned, they must already have been defeated or if not have withdrawn back to their original position across the river at Duyinzeik to await a Jap attack.

I made two decisions. I would walk north up the Salween for some miles before turning west, intending to rejoin our forces well behind the front lines of the opposing armies. The second decision was to start off on the firm ground between the water and the river bank. I did not know how far up river the firm ground would extend; but as it had not rained for six months or so, there must have been a good chance of a lot of firm ground. This decision meant however that I could not start until it was dark, as I had to negotiate the ferry terminus opposite Pa-an. In daylight I would also have been in full view from across the river, although I might have been prepared to risk this because there was no longer any reason for anyone on the other side of the river to watch my side.

In a later chapter I will analyse where I went wrong and the reasons for my failure to rejoin our forces. This and the subsequent chapter consist of a narrative of my actual experiences over the next three days.

As soon as it was dusk, I walked down the ravine past the spot where the wounded Jerry Dyer had lain and turned left up river towards the ferry. I was pleased to find a number of bushes growing out of and below the river bank. These would provide me with cover when necessary. I waited until it was actually dark before leaving cover into view from the ferry terminus. There was quite a bit of activity on the road which at this point ran beside the river from the ferry terminus before moving a bit inland. Nevertheless I was hopeful of being able to get past the ferry terminus along the shore in the darkness. I knew that no moon was expected for several hours. I made a start; but suddenly the whole area was flooded with light. The Japs had erected arc lights. I dropped down beside a boat, which was fortunately lying there on the dry ground, just before a man ran past only a few feet from me towards the water's edge. I saw a boat with lights crossing from Pa-an. I waited for a while crouched down beside the boat hidden from the arc lights. I hoped that when the boat load from Pa-an had emptied, the Japs might switch off the lights. But this did not happen. I could also hear a number of voices. I judged it too risky to go any further as long as the lights were on. I was fast becoming anxious at my lack of progress. The arc lights and the activity at the ferry might last all night. I decided that I could not wait any longer and ran back out of the floodlit area. I was not spotted.

I then decided to adopt my second choice plan. This was to walk across country using my compass in as direct a line as possible to a point on the river Donthami north of Kyettuywethaung, but well to the south of Duyinzeik, which I had decided to avoid. I hoped that we would have troops at Kyettuywethaung as had been the case at the time of my abortive boat trip. I was a strong swimmer; and to swim the river would have presented no problems. It was nearer as the crow flies than Duyinzeik and in fact the nearest point where I could have expected our troops to be.

I walked briskly back past my ravine and soon left the river. I found myself in part of the sprawling village of Kuzeik. There was no movement. I had spent so long trying to get past the ferry terminus that from the sounds it seemed that all the villagers were now asleep. I decided not to waste any more time by going back. I threaded my way unobserved quickly and quietly through the village. I soon realised that it was impossible to walk in a fixed line from my compass as taught to us in training in India. I had to deviate along paths to avoid thick jungle or patches of impassable paddy fields (consisting of muddy water through which rice was growing). I used my luminous compass frequently to try to keep generally in the right direction. But inevitably the paths forced me off my line, sometimes even at right angles. I could not read my map as it was pitch dark. All of this slowed me up.

Nevertheless I had been making reasonable progress when I suddenly saw a swaying lantern catching me up from behind. I dropped down at once into some damp thick grass below the path, which in fact formed the bank of a paddy field. I crouched there head-down on the edge of the paddy field for a long time listening to the sound of file after file of Jap troops marching in silence a few feet above my head.

This was not the only occasion when I was delayed by having to take cover to avoid Jap troops, always led by a man with a lamp. I assumed that the men with lamps were Burmans showing the way to the Japs. None came so close again.

Later, still in pitch darkness, I was walking cautiously along a path crossing through the outskirts of a sleeping village. It was some time since I had run into any Japs. When I rounded a corner in the village I suddenly stopped dead in my tracks. Not far in front I saw a lighted cigarette, not a Burmese cheroot. When the smoker drew on the cigarette I could make out a dark shape sitting on the steps of the hut and it looked to me as if he was wearing headgear of some sort. Whether or not that was the case, I knew that Burmese villagers never smoke cigarettes. I moved quickly to my right and dropped down behind a low bush. There was a loud challenge in a language and tone of voice I was to know so well in the ensuing years. This was followed by quite a long pause. I started to move slowly and quietly away from the path. Suddenly I heard the 'plop' of a stone hitting the ground some way to my left. Then another - nearer. I was momentarily reminded of the most exciting episode in my school boy reading - the tapping of blind Pew's stick on the road as he approached the Inn where young Jim Hawkins and his mother were cowering. I listened to the stones 'plopping' into low bushes or onto the ground, with pauses between, but nearer each time. I knew that a stone striking my body would make a different sound. I remained crouched on the balls of my feet, absolutely still, with my pistol ready to aim and fire. I was poised to move swiftly and quietly to the left the moment I was struck by a stone, but keeping my balance so that I could fire at the flash of a gun or a Jap charging out of the darkness. I would then run for it. But once again my luck held. One stone landed close to me to my left, one on the right and then one or two more further right. Nothing more happened. After a time I moved quietly away from the village.

After the moon had risen I was able to walk less slowly. I reached more open country. I noticed a rocky hill, unusual in such a flat terrain. I decided to climb this and rest until dawn. I would then have a view over the countryside which I hoped would enable me to identify my position on my map. Once it was daylight, I was optimistic about reaching the river before long. I was pretty sure that the Jap troops, whom I had encountered earlier, were marching north. If this was so, there must be a good chance of few, if any, being as far south as that part of the Donthami where I was intending to cross.

At the foot of the hill, there was a grassy open space among some trees. I found a very steep rocky path, or more likely the dry bed of what would be a stream in the monsoon season, leading from the glade up the hill. I climbed this until I came to a flat spot beneath the overhanging cover of a large rock. I lay down; and I fell fast asleep. I was of course very short of sleep. My last had been on the previous night and had only been for about two hours, perhaps less, before the Japs attacked. My hiding place up the side of the ravine had been too uncomfortable to allow me to do more than doze occasionally during the afternoon.

I was awakened by roars of male and shrieks of female laughter. I noticed that the sun was quite well up in the sky. My assessment was that there were at least two couples in the glade below me. I assumed that the men were Japs and the girls Burmese. From the girlish laughter, which emanated from time to time, there was no question of rape. All were enjoying themselves except me for whom it was utterly disastrous.

The party stayed in the glade below until late afternoon.

Sometimes there was silence and my hopes rose that they had gone. But the voices started again, although more quietly. Clearly they had been sleeping it off. There was no way I could climb down from where I was without being seen.

When I was eventually able to leave there was little daylight left. The terrain consisted largely of low scrubland and paddy fields. This was about what I had expected from the study of my map. Unfortunately I had been unable to identify my exact position. It soon became pitch dark; and my progress of course slowed. I was very hungry and thirsty. Another night of uncertain progress loomed ahead. I decided that I must risk entering a Burmese house to fill up my empty water bottle and grab some edible food. We had all had our suspicions that the Burmese were helping the Japs. My own suspicions had been increased by my experiences over the last twenty four hours. Nevertheless I knew of no concrete evidence. The Burmese villagers had not seemed unfriendly. That is when I had noticed them! In any event there might be a chance of my encountering a villager, male or female, who would be sympathetic to my predicament. Unfortunately there were no isolated houses. All were in villages. I selected a house on the outskirts of the village. I climbed up a few steps into the living room. The startled occupant gave me no chance to make any request. He started jabbering at the top of his voice. I stuck my pistol up against his ribs. He only jabbered more loudly. I felt that I could not risk staying any longer. I grabbed a handful of cooked rice from a pot and ran off with it in my pocket.

CHAPTER V

CAPTURED

As dawn broke I climbed a tree and scanned the open horizon hoping at last to see the river. It was not in sight. But what I did see standing beneath the tree and staring up at me was a Burmese boy. I smiled at him, putting my index finger to my lips and indicating in sign language that he must not give me away. He ran off. Realistically I knew that there was no hope of his keeping quiet. In any event the Burmese villager from whom I had taken the rice would have alerted the Japs.

I pressed on, all the time listening for the search party which I considered to be inevitable and also taking care not to be seen again by a villager. When I heard voices and the beating of bushes in the distance I started looking for a hiding place. Not for the first time I found an excellent one. This was in a thicket with only one possible entrance and this was invisible from the path. Twice during the next few hours they passed along the path outside my hiding place and on both occasions the noise of nearby searching stopped. I sensed that someone was staring into the thicket. I remained absolutely still. The searchers moved on.

I knew that my situation was now desperate. I decided to sleep and make one last effort as soon as night fell. At about 4.00pm I heard searchers returning nearby. I was so confident that my hiding place was secure that I had grown careless. Unaware, while dozing, I had left one leg visible to a searcher finding the entrance and looking into the thicket from there. I was fully awakened by a shout and rolled over onto my back to see a man of Asiatic visage, naked to the waist, kneeling in front of me with a jungle knife poised, quivering, to plunge into my heart. Fortunately, he then decided to

do a slower demolition job and re-aligned his knife to strike a softer part of my anatomy. This gave me a chance to act. I shot out my left arm pointing into the dark thicket, following its direction with my head and eyes. I shouted "look over there you................"
He took his eyes off me to look where I was pointing. Immediately with my right arm I whipped out my pistol on which I had been partially lying and which had been hidden from his sight. He realised his danger, dropped his knife and grabbed my pistol just as I had it pointed at his face. I pulled the trigger. The pistol misfired.[4] Before I could pull the trigger again, he forced it away from his face to my left. He was far too strong and wrenched the pistol away from me. During the struggle he shouted to the outside the thicket. One of them shouted back. He then made signs that I should get up and go outside.

I scrambled out of the darkness of the thicket into the late afternoon sunshine. There were about six men standing outside. They were wearing only shorts and light footwear. Each had a jungle knife. They stared at me curiously. I suppose I could well have been the first white man they had ever seen. Surprisingly, they were not unfriendly. I asked if they were Japanese. One nodded agreement. We set off along a path in a group. We had not gone far when the Jap on my left politely tapped my watch and pointed to himself. The terms of the Geneva Convention flashed through my mind, but I had the sense to hand it to him with a smile. This was the signal for a search of my pockets and knapsack by two or three of the others. They found only my map, compass and the last few grains of the handful of rice which I had been keeping for nightfall. This caused great amusement. I even felt I detected a sympathetic note in their guttural exclamations. I responded in a smiling friendly way. They gave me water and indicated that there would be food for me later.

Any relief I may have felt in the improvement in my condition was short-lived. We reached a clearing where we met some more

Japs. One was obviously in command. He wore a T-shirt and shorts; he brandished a sword and started to shout. He ordered my captors to surround me and to hold the points of their knives against my body. This they did, fortunately not over-enthusiastically and without drawing blood. This horrid little man then jumped around in front of me shouting and waving his sword in my face. The only word I understood and which was continually repeated was "JAPAN." I bit back the defiant shout of "ENGLAND" which so nearly came out. Instead, I smiled at him, a smile intended to be friendly but calm and dignified - although I expect I only produced my usual grin. Certainly it achieved nothing.

The 'tamasha'[5] continued. He carried on waving his sword in front of my face and shouting. At his command they all applied pressure with the points of their knives. I steeled myself to face them with dignity and to show no trace of fear. Apart from the obligation to behave as a British Officer should, I felt instinctively that my only chance of survival lay in earning their respect by my conduct. [This appraisal was to a certain extent corroborated by the experience of Brigadier Hobson (the Senior British Officer in Rangoon Jail) in very similar circumstances. He could speak Japanese and unlike me understood what was being said. It was made clear to him by words and sword action that he was to be decapitated. After a "tamasha" not unlike mine he was informed that, as he had "shown good spirit," he would be spared].

I do not know what saved me from being decapitated or carved up with knives (another of their disagreeable habits at the time). There is only one certain fact. My life depended on the whim of one singularly unpleasant member of an unpredictable race. However that may be, the 'tamasha' terminated and I was put in the back of a bullock cart with my hands tied in front of me. My escorts and I were driven to a village. On the way an English speaking Japanese journalist, who had visited England, suddenly appeared, jumped on board the bullock cart and greeted me by

42

smacking my face - a harbinger of things to come. He regaled me with an account of Japanese successes in Malaya and elsewhere (Singapore fell next day). By the time he jumped off he was more friendly. He even gave me a parting present of six raw eggs. I ate one but did not enjoy it. I saved the rest until we reached a village where we were all given a meal. I mixed the five raw eggs with my rice, as the cook refused to cook them for me. It was my first meal for seventy-five hours. I have seldom enjoyed one more. Without realising it, I had learned one of the rules for survival as a Japanese prisoner - 'live for the present and do not worry about the future.'

My journey continued after supper. Sometime during the night we arrived at the village of Kuzeik through which I had threaded my way unobserved in the early hours of my attempt to rejoin our forces two nights before.

I was left alone to sleep well into the morning. In the afternoon I was ferried across the Salween to Pa-an.

PART II

A PRISONER OF THE JAPANESE

Men that are men again; who goes home?
Tocsin and triumpeter! Who goes home?
For there's blood on the field and blood on the foam
And blood on the body when Man goes home.
And a voice valedictory ... Who is for Victory?
Who is for Liberty? Who goes home?'

Who goes home?   G K Chesterton

CHAPTER VI

PA-AN JAIL

I was escorted through the streets of Pa-an to the front of the jail. I heard an excited shout in Urdu, "Coubrough Sahib is here." This was not exactly an earth-shattering piece of news. The arrival of a captive Second Lieutenant Coubrough was hardly comparable with say the sight of the US 7th Cavalry galloping to save a besieged garrison. But it did have the effect of three smiling faces appearing immediately on the first floor balcony to greet me warmly. They were those of my fellow officers, Captain Hugh Mercer, Captain Bill Cayley and Second Lieutenant Jake Jervis. I was taken upstairs to join them in their room.

They gave me the sad news that Toots was lying severely wounded in a nearby building. They had each been allowed to visit him in turn; but entreaties for proper medical care had fallen on deaf ears. All the rest of our wounded had been killed by the Japs. (Toots had been saved at the last minute by the whim of a Jap officer).

They themselves had been well-treated. They had been completely segregated however from our Indian troops, who included the Medical Officer (a Captain) and four VCO's. (Viceroy Commissioned Officers, equivalent to Warrant Officers in the British Army).

I was allowed to pay a short visit to Toots. I was so upset by his condition that I walked back through the Jap Guardroom without acknowledging their presence. This was greeted by a roar of rage; but I was not beaten up as I would have been later in Rangoon Jail for such conduct.

It was not until I reached Moulmein Jail that I sat down to

reflect on what had happened to me and what the future might hold. For the rest of that day, although saddened by Toots' condition and concerned about the fate of the rest of the battalion, of which the others had no information, I found it wonderful to be in the company of friends after the last few days on my own.

CHAPTER VII

BOAT TRIP FROM PA-AN TO MOULMEIN

The next morning the four of us embarked on a large motor boat together with some thirty or so Indian POW's. We were in the stern of the boat, separated from our troops who were all up forward. In between, two Jap soldiers, each armed with a rifle, were seated facing us across the open space in the middle of the boat. There was a Burmese boatman steering the boat.

After two nights sleep and plenty of food, my batteries were now fully recharged. I was standing in the corner of the boat in front of the stern on the starboard side, watching the slowly passing scenery with great interest. As previously mentioned, I had made a close study of this part of the Salween on my map before my abortive pleasure boat trip. I was able to recognise certain features.

By early afternoon we had not reached the confluence of the rivers Salween and Donthami. It was very hot. I suddenly noticed that one of the Japs had fallen asleep and was not even holding his rifle. This was propped up beside him only about three or four paces from where I was standing. The other Jap looked pretty sleepy too; but he was gripping his rifle. I said quietly to Hugh Mercer, who was standing next to me:

"You know we could easily 'pakaro'[6] this boat."
This was only intended as an observation and not a suggestion for action, although I would have followed any lead and played my part. Hugh, who had been the adjutant and was the senior of us, treated it, however, as a serious suggestion. He turned it down. He was absolutely right to do so. I shall explain why. But at the time, I remember reflecting that I might have received a different answer

48

from one or more of the 7 Baluch Officers who were not present.

In theory, in the circumstances I have outlined above, it would have been perfectly possible to seize the boat, proceed the short distance down the Salween to the confluence with the Donthami, disembark on the north side of the Donthami and disperse into small groups, not so very far from the Thaton/Duyinzeik area where we expected our forces to be - without the Japs having any idea what had happened. Of course the further the boat went up the Donthami the greater would have been the risk. There were no boats on the Salween other than ours which was being used to ferry batches of POW's from Pa-an to Moulmein. If some Burmese villagers should see a struggle or hear a shot, they would have no radio or other means of communication with the Japs.

That is the theory. No doubt there would have been highly-trained, determined troops on either side during the war who would have taken advantage of such an opportunity. (One excludes the Japanese as they would never have allowed themselves to be taken prisoner at all).

It is however no reflection on any person in that boat and certainly not on Hugh Mercer, (who was granted a Regular Commission after the war and made his mark in the early days of the SAS) to state that in practice we would not have found it at all easy to seize the boat. Decisive action would have had to be taken at once. Any half hearted effort would have inevitably ended in a messy failure. Even if we had succeeded in seizing the boat and had landed unobserved by the Japs on the north bank of the Donthami, our problems would only have started. We were no longer the disciplined unit which had repulsed the Japanese attacks for so long during the battle of Pa-an. We would have become a rag-bag of escaped prisoners of war, who had recently experienced the traumas of defeat and capture.

In fact the problems would have been far worse than we could have anticipated. It was February 16th. Unknown to us, our forces had completed their withdrawal from the Duyinzeik - Thaton line on February 15th. Over the following ten days or so, they were continually being outflanked and withdrawing until they reached the Sittang River, and blew up the bridge.

Although a prisoner of war has a duty to try to escape, there were in this case other considerations. The lives of the whole boatload would have been at risk. Unless there was a real chance of a substantial number succeeding in rejoining our forces, I have no doubt, looking at the situation dispassionately over fifty years later, that such a risk should never have been taken. It would have been quite unjustifiable to condemn such a large number of soldiers, many of whom had fought so gallantly during the battle, to the tender mercies of a pitiless enemy. Hugh Mercer was quite right.

CHAPTER VIII

MOULMEIN JAIL

16th February to 25th June 1942

A.   A time for reflection

During my several months in Moulmein Jail I had plenty of time to reflect on what had happened to me and to speculate on what the future might hold.

I fear that my first thoughts were not exactly praiseworthy. They were that I was alive and well and extremely lucky to be so. As with so many who were in action in the war, I had had my share of near misses and close calls, both before, during and after the battle, in which to be wounded was virtually a death sentence (Toots being the only exception). But to no one could the 'Grim Reaper' have come so close and then passed by as he did to me in the late afternoon of 14th February.

After I had arrived in Moulmein Jail, I felt that for me the fighting was over. Although circumstances might change in the future, for the present survival was the name of the game.

As for the future, I remembered the Coubrough family motto 'Comme je trouve' engraved on the gold cufflinks which my grandmother had given me. (Heaven knows where the motto came from). I was realistic enough to appreciate that the war was likely to continue for some years; and I was prepared to face up to this. I never doubted our ultimate victory. I was not one of those who believed that the Japanese would kill all their prisoners. The events of the last few weeks had given me the confidence to believe that I could handle whatever the future and the Japanese might have in

51

store for me.

My morale did however receive a 'jolt' when we were joined by the officers captured after the Sittang bridge was blown up. These included Lieutenant Colonel Henry Power CO of the Dogras. The Colonel was greeted by a barrage of questions which all boiled-down to one crucial question "What happened to you on the night of the 11th/12th February?" After he had replied, not entirely to our satisfaction, he went on to tell us that five of our officers had succeeded in reaching Duyinzeik. They had arrived separately from each other over a period of twenty-four hours or so. They had all followed the line of the road.

Like the others, I was delighted to learn that the five of them were all safe. I was, however, disappointed to learn that my appreciation of the situation had been wrong. The Japs did not follow the retreating Dogras up the road to Duyinzeik. Naturally I felt at the time that, having avoided detection in the initial search, I also could have succeeded in making my way back along the road to Duyinzeik. But I decided that no useful purpose would be served by dwelling on this.

Over the years I have discussed their experiences with one or two of those who reached Duyinzeik safely. I have recently studied various maps of the area. I am now able to analyse my actions and assess my performance.

Despite the fact that the Japs did not advance along the road, none of the five had found it easy to leave the battlefield after the battle was over and cover the fifteen miles to Duyinzeik. It would have been more difficult for me than the others as I was down by the river and cut off by that part of the road parallel to the river, which was in constant use by the Japs. I would have had to leave much later. Nevertheless I have no doubt that given reasonable luck I could have 'made it' to Duyinzeik before the Dogras withdrew.

I will deal first with my fateful decision to avoid the road to

52

Duyinzeik and instead to try to start off walking north up the Salween. This was of course partly prompted by my position down by the river. It was also due to my assessment referred to in Chapter IV that the Japs would wish to seize the only road from Pa-an to Thaton. This assessment was the product of our thinking at the time. In *Defeat into Victory* Field Marshall Slim writes: 'The 17th Indian Division. had been trained and equipped, like all Indian Army Divisions, for desert warfare in the Middle East. Its transport was mechanical and except in open country it was incapable of operating off a road.' At that stage in the Burma Campaign, I do not believe that any of the senior officers in the 17th Indian Division expected the Japanese Army to ignore the road to Duyinzeik and instead to move northwards through the jungle. [It is also the case that John Randle made the same appreciation of the situation as I did. He was forced to change his chosen route by factors which did not apply to me]. In fact it was actually fortunate for me that I was forced back when I was unable to pass the ferry terminus opposite Pa-an. If I had continued, I would have been moving in the same direction as the Japanese army.

My second choice to aim for a point on the Donthami to the north of Kyettuywethaung but well to the south of Duyinzeik had more by good luck than judgement, a much better prospect of success. It is a fact that no large force of Japs moved along either bank of the Donthami.

I have in my possession a sketch map showing the dispositions of our forces along the Donthami at that time. To the south of the Dogras at Duyinzeik were 1/7 Gurkhas and to the south of them the 4th Battalion of the Burma Rifles. This battalion was positioned only a little to the north of the point on the Donthami at which I was aiming. If I had succeeded in swimming the Donthami, I would probably have walked northwards along the west bank of the river towards Duyinzeik. There must have then been a chance of my being picked up by a Burma Rifle patrol.

Failing this, I would have reached their position which was never attacked.

In fact I must have been quite near the Donthami when I was captured. I was a number of hours in the bullock cart before reaching Kuzeik. So I clearly covered an appreciable distance. I know that I was to the north of Kyettuywethaung as otherwise I would have seen the lakes to the east of that village (see Map 2). I may however have been further north and nearer to Duyinzeik than I had planned.

On an assessment of my performance from the time when I climbed into my hiding place as the Japs started to search my vicinity until my capture, there are two plus points:

1.   My determination not to give myself up to the Japanese but to fight my way out if necessary remained constant until the end.

2.   In moments of danger, I found I remained cool. I was able to think clearly and to decide at once what action to take.

But oh dear there were so many minus factors in my performance that I do not know where to start! I have already analysed my reasons for taking the wrong decision to avoid the road to Duyinzeik. A further disadvantage of not moving along the line of either the road or the river was that my compass and map reading skills became of primary importance. In fact my experience of these arts in the jungle was very limited. I grossly underestimated the difficulty of finding my way through the jungle at night without a torch to read my map. It was essential that I moved as quickly as possible. Our forces might well withdraw. My performance was likely to deteriorate due to weakness caused by lack of food and water. Having experienced the difficulty of moving through the jungle at night in the right direction and having been slowed down by the movement of Jap troops, I should never have allowed myself to fall asleep when I decided quite sensibly to rest. It is no good complaining about my undoubted bad luck when the Japs chose the glade below me for their 'petting party.' I should never have been there in the first place. I should have made certain that I used the early light, when I could read my map, at a time when there would be few, possibly hostile, Burmans around. The further I walked, the less likely I was to run into Japs. I might well have reached the Donthami that morning.

Looking back dispassionately over fifty years later and with the knowledge of the movements of the two armies which took place at the time, it is clear to me that once I had taken the crucial decision, which was wrong but certainly understandable, to avoid the road, my prospects were pretty 'dicey.' Considering my lack of training and experience of map reading in the jungle I did not do too badly (particularly in the early stages) until I allowed myself to fall asleep. If I had kept awake or even if the Japs had chosen somewhere else for their 'petting party,' I might even have 'made it.' If I had, it would have been considered a fine performance. As it was I failed, but I did my best. No one other than me suffered on account of my failure.

What is certain beyond any doubt, however, is that, if I had succeeded, my attitude would have been quite different. I had learnt what war really was. I realised the necessity for me to adopt a more serious, less amateurish approach. I would have tried hard to build on my undoubted enthusiasm and any other positive attributes I may have possessed, such as latent ability, to improve my performance as an officer in the Battalion, which had to recover from the trauma of defeat before it could fight effectively against such a formidable enemy. I would not have wanted to be anywhere else. But it was not to be.

B.   Life in the Jail

On 6th March those British and Indian troops taken prisoner when the Sittang Bridge was blown up reached the jail.

They were divided between three blocks, the British officers in one, to which the four of us had been removed the day they arrived, the British warrant officers and other ranks in another and Indian officers, VCOs and other ranks in a third. There was also a building used as a hospital to which Toots, who had been ferried down from Pa-an with another boat load of Baluch prisoners was sent. We never saw him in Moulmein Jail.

During the eighteen days on our own we had been locked in solitary cells but allowed to talk to each other. Our Japanese Commandant, who unfortunately was replaced when the Sittang prisoners arrived, was quite friendly when we saw him. In the evening we were allowed to sit outside our cell block in the fresh air for thirty minutes or so. On one or two occasions he joined us, offered round Japanese cigarettes and chatted with us in excellent English in a friendly way. Unfortunately I never again met a Japanese officer who treated us in the same way.

I remember one unusual occasion during that period. One evening the Commandant informed us that a Japanese general would come to inspect us the next day. He did not speak English but did speak French. He would like to talk in French to one of us. We all said that we were not French speakers, but as the Commandant insisted, Hugh Mercer suggested that as I had left school last I should be the one to talk to the General in French. I disagreed strongly but the next day the Commandant appeared outside my cell with an impressive-looking Japanese officer. The latter asked me "Parlez-vous francais?" I intended to inform him that my French was very bad. Unfortunately I used the words "Bahut kharab," Urdu being the foreign language I had been battling to learn for the past year, instead of "très mauvais." Understandably the General looked at me with incomprehension. Unexpectedly he then smiled and moved away. Jervis, who had listened to the conversation in the next cell, thought it a huge joke. When we were joined by the Sittang prisoners he lost no time in regaling them with the story of my conversation with the Japanese General. [It occurs to me that it is possible that the General was Lt-General Sakurai, Commander of 33rd Division who defeated us in the Battle of Pa-an. In *Burma 1942: The Japanese Invasion* he is described as 'outstanding' and it is stated that he spoke French having spent two years as military attaché in Paris].

From the time of the arrival of the Sittang prisoners we were no longer locked in our cells but allowed to move around the building. This included an upper storey reached up a wooden staircase. There was a view over the top of the prison walls. One could see the tops of houses, swaying palm trees and a golden pagoda. ['The old Moulmein Pagoda, lookin' eastward to the sea'? We argued amongst ourselves that Rudyard Kipling had got it wrong and the pagoda was facing westward to the sea]. One could also see the shimmering waters of the Gulf of Martban in the distance. It was my favourite place.

Although we were never hit by any of the guards, their attitude was unfriendly and at times threatening. Frequently the Jail would be visited by Japanese troops passing through Moulmein. They would stand and stare silently at us. Usually we took no notice and carried on with what we were doing. But on one occasion I called out "You will find the monkey house upstairs." One of them shouted back "KURA," glaring at me ferociously. I have to admit that I was glad that we were behind a locked iron gate and that they were not accompanied by one of our guards with a key. Of course, if we had been in Rangoon Jail we would have been standing silently to attention while the Japs studied us.

On one occasion our building had a different kind of visitor - equally unwelcome. Someone observed a large snake curled up and probably asleep in an empty cell. Two of us, each armed with a stick, decided to drive it out. We hurried along the corridor and dashed through the open door into the cell, shouting "charge." We stopped dead. We watched transfixed as a cobra, one of the

57

deadliest snakes on earth, raised up its hooded head right in front of us. The snake then uncoiled and disappeared quickly thorough he grating - much to our relief.

One of the few pleasant aspects of life in Moulmein Jail was that we were sometimes marched out of the Jail to an open air public wash place, always vacated by the locals at the time.

The main aspect of life in Moulmein Jail was that (after the first eighteen days on our own) we were simply not given enough to eat. We had two meals a day. In the morning we had a partially filled mess tin of rice and haricot-type beans and in the evening a similar amount of rice and vegetable marrow. There was no salt with either. We were all permanently hungry.

After we had been in the Jail for some time, we were joined by four of a mixed party of English and Australians, who had escaped from Singapore in a sailing boat after the capitulation. Their performance in reaching Southern Burma, which they had hoped was India, was remarkable. It was also extremely interesting for us to hear what they had to say about the Malayan campaign and the fall of Singapore. One of their number was a doctor, Captain Kilgour RAMC. As subsequently recorded, he died in solitary confinement in Rangoon Jail. He was, in my opinion, a man of considerable calibre and his death was a great loss to us all. He could well have been a hero of Rangoon Jail like Major Ramsay RAMC.

CHAPTER IX

SEA VOYAGE FROM MOULMEIN TO RANGOON

On the 25th June without any prior warning together with the BORs (British other ranks) from another Block we were paraded and driven by lorry to the harbour. There we embarked on a cargo boat, of perhaps some three thousand tons. Except for the very sick, who were allowed to remain on deck, the rest of us were ordered to climb down a rope ladder into a hold. The rope ladder was then pulled up and the trap door closed.

There was one bare electric light. By this we saw that the sides of the hold were lined with sacks. We discovered that these contained slabs of 'jagri' (a form of sugar). In the centre of the hold there were several empty rectangular kerosene or petrol cans (with sharp edges) for use as latrines. We climbed on to the 'jagri' sacks which were not uncomfortable. We opened one and at first enjoyed eating the 'jagri.' None of us had eaten any sweet food for many weeks. But this soon palled and made us thirsty. Unfortunately the heat engendered by the bodies caused the 'jagri' to start melting. The sticky moisture permeated through the sacks. Fortunately I was lying on an army greatcoat which had been issued to me on arrival at Moulmein Jail for use as a blanket.

From time to time, the hatch door was opened and a rope lowered. This was used to lift up the full cans of urine and excreta to the deck above for emptying and return. Several of the BORs were suffering from severe dysentery. The use of these makeshift latrines was a nightmare for these unfortunate men. The only ventilation in the hold was through the trap door which was kept closed except when the cans were being lifted up. The heat and

MAP 4

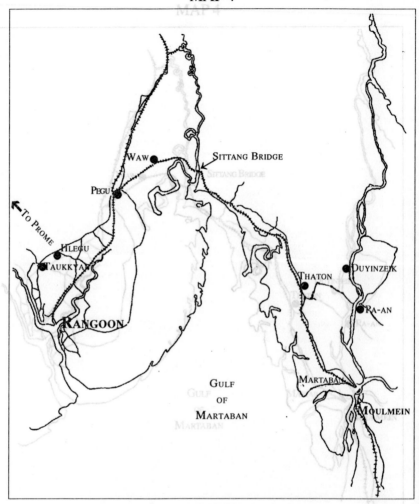

AREA SURROUNDING GULF OF MARTABAN
(RELEVANT TO CHAPTERS IX TO XIV)

the foul smell increased as the hours went by. We had no means of telling the time, although we could see that night had fallen when the trap door was lifted.

We had no information as to our destination. Most of us expected it to be Singapore. We only hoped that the voyage would not last long. In addition to enduring increasingly vile unhealthy conditions, we were aware that if the ship was the object of an allied air or sea attack, the hold would be a death trap for us.

Eventually the ship stopped moving. There were sounds of activity on the deck above us. The rope ladder was lowered and we climbed up on deck. It was daylight and raining hard. Through the murky light I saw rising above the other buildings the golden Dome of the Schwedagon Pagoda. We were in Rangoon.

We were marched through the streets of Rangoon until we reached the main jail. There we were greeted by the Commandant Captain Koshima and his second in command, 'The Little Corporal,' about both of whom I shall write more in subsequent chapters. We were lined up and ordered to bow to the Japs. Those who did not do this promptly were shouted at and had their faces slapped by the Jap guards. Although on this occasion the face slapping was not particularly severe, it marked a turning point in our treatment. It was the first time any officer had been hit. We realised that we were now under Japanese military discipline.

We were taken off to solitary cells throughout the jail. That evening as I reflected on the events of the last two days, I was comparatively cheerful, despite the fact that I was in solitary confinement and appeared likely to be knocked around a bit. There were however two compensating factors for which I was grateful:
1.   In the afternoon, having had no food (apart from the 'jagri') since leaving Moulmein Jail, I had been extremely relieved to see two BORs appearing at my cell door carrying containers of food. My mess-tins were filled not only with rice but with a stew consisting of meat and fresh vegetables. This was a tremendous improvement

61

on the debilitating diet given to us in Moulmein Jail.

2.   I was no longer in that stinking hold, which could have become a death trap, on the ship, but on dry land in Burma. This was nearer to our forces than any other country conquered by the Japanese and thus likely to be liberated first.

But there was still to be a sting in the tail of that day. During that night I was rudely awakened from the deep sleep into which I had fallen. My body was covered by a swarm of ants crawling all over me. I leaped off my iron bedstead. In the moonlight I saw a trail of red ants stretching from the base of one of the legs of the bed, up which they were climbing, to the cell door and then across the verandah outside. My cell was on the first floor and the ants had come all the way from the ground below to sample the remains of the melted 'jagri' on my greatcoat. I had quite a job getting rid of the ants and of all remaining traces of the 'jagri.' The whole episode gave me 'the creeps.'

THE SCHWEDAGON PAGODA

CHAPTER X

Solitary Confinement

26 June to 8 September 1942

When we were taken off to our solitary cells, I was separated from the rest of the officers brought from Moulmein. I do not know why. Perhaps I was standing at the end of the line. Although I was unaware of this at the time, the others were all put in cells in the main solitary block. I was taken to a cell in the Punishment Block (as named by the British). This consisted of two buildings, each comprising two storeys of about ten cells on each floor. While I was there, none on the ground floor were in use, nor were those on the first floor ever fully occupied.

The other occupants had all been captured after the fall of Rangoon. To my left was an empty cell and then one occupied at the end by Brigadier Hobson. In July, he was exchanged with Colonel Mackenzie RAMC who had been placed in the main solitary block with the others on our arrival from Moulmein. I shall be writing about both later on. To my right there were two empty cells and then one occupied by a captain in the Madras Sappers and Miners. For a time the two cells between us were each occupied by a private in the Royal Inniskilling Fusiliers. I never found out why they were there, because I could not understand a word my neighbour said. Eventually I correctly interpreted the words "Hae ye a leet?" I replied "No. I do not have any matches." Thereafter our attempts at conversation ceased.

In any event talking was strictly forbidden. I had been told of this by my neighbours and of the necessity to stand to attention at all times and bow for Jap guards. In fact the punishment cells were situated on the outskirts of the prison, well away from the guard house. Unlike those in the main solitary block, to where I was moved later, we were left very much alone. We were seldom visited by guards except on the following occasions:

1.   Our morning ablutions, when we emptied our 'benjo cans' (urine and excreta) and poured water over ourselves, using our mess tins from a tap. (Nowadays this exercise would be called 'slopping out').

2.   Our morning and evening meals, which were brought to our cells by two BORs always accompanied by a guard.

3.   Sporadic visits by the Commandant's interpreter leaving and collecting questionnaires.

I had a view of the gate into the compound from the darkness of my cell and so there was plenty of time to stand to attention. Unfortunately our seclusion had its disadvantages. I was caught twice, on both occasions by the guard appearing from the back of the two buildings.

The first time was by a powerfully built squat guard, who always walked with his head thrust forward. He was subsequently called 'Humpy' or 'The ape.' I heard a furious shout and leaped from my bed to my cell door to stand to attention and bow. It was too late. He mounted the steps on to the verandah, opened my cell door and ordered me to step out. He then hit me across the face. His hands were open, not clenched, but he brought his blows up powerfully from low down. Each one half stunned me, knocking me sideways. This was immediately corrected by a blow from the other side - and so on. All the time he shouted at me. It was by far the most severe face slapping I was to receive during my captivity.

The second time was by a guard whom we subsequently called 'Blackie.' He heard me talking to Colonel Mackenzie. I was again called out of my cell on to the verandah. He hit me on the calves of my legs and on my upper arms with a stick. When he tired of this activity, he did not scrape the point of his stick along

64

the weals, as the little corporal did to Brigadier Hobson on one occasion. Instead his eyes alighted on the gym shoes (lightly made but heavier in the heel) which I was wearing, having acquired them on our leaving Moulmein Jail. He ordered me to take one off. He then hit me on the face with the heel. This hurt more than I expected and I let out an involuntary exclamation - more of surprise than anything else. That did it. He shouted and screamed at me, thrashing me across the face with the heel of my gym shoe for quite some time. I never wore the gym shoes again, consigning them to my benjo can the next morning. I walked around barefoot for the rest of my time as a prisoner.

I have been asked how I passed my time in solitary. I tried to keep fit by walking round the cell which was only about fourteen feet by eight. The only book I possessed was a slim volume of poems by Sir Henry Newbolt, one of the few books we possessed in Moulmein Jail. It was stirring stuff - 'Drake's Drum,' 'The Fighting Temeraire' etc. Unfortunately I had ceased appreciating this sort of verse before I left my prep school. But some of his poems were different. [In a later chapter I relate an episode when this book of poems reappeared in 3 Block].

But in reality most of my time while I was in the punishment cells was spent in answering the questionnaires with which Captain Koshima bombarded us. On the face of it they were designed to obtain military information, but they were also probably for the dual purpose of humiliating us and boosting the ego of Captain Koshima.

I enjoyed answering these questionnaires. It gave me the opportunity to exercise my mind, which to me was every bit as important in coping with the pressures of solitary confinement as exercising my body. My objective was to answer the questions in such a way that they disclosed no information which could possibly be of any value without giving the Japs any excuse to discipline me. For instance I remember one question: "I am the Japanese

Commander invading India; what can I expect to find?" My reply was: "the roads will be dusty except in the monsoon season when they will be wet." I believe we were meant to write essays; but I always kept my replies short.

Another reason why I enjoyed receiving these questionnaires was that I established some rapport with the Commandant's interpreter who delivered and received them back. He was a young ex-university student, bespectacled and of poor physique. Despite his position as the Commandant's interpreter he was only a junior private and had his face slapped by his superiors in rank (i.e. pretty well all the guards) from time to time. During the period of my time in 'solitary,' he was the only Jap who ever smiled at me and sometimes he exchanged a few friendly words.

However, on the 13th August 1942 he handed me a document which I did not enjoy reading. It contained 14 paragraphs of justification for the Japanese attack on the USA and Britain, it detailed their military successes to-date and ended up by offering a well-paid job broadcasting for the Japs in 'the cherry blossoming country.' I attach a photocopy of this document (Appendix A). This 'ridiculous nonsense' made me seethe with anger. I was particularly incensed at the statement that 'your people seemed to become war-prisoners shamelessly.' During the two and a half days endeavouring to rejoin our forces after the Battle of Pa-an, it had never once entered my head to surrender to the Japanese; and I had tried to shoot the Jap soldier who overpowered me. I set out below a copy of the counterfoil attached to the last page:

REPLY
You are requested to indicate your willingness to broadcast by stating 'yes' or 'no' in the space below

Signed ....

I wrote 'no' with satisfaction and signed it.

A day or so later the interpreter came to my cell and handed me a piece of paper on which was written:

'You are given 10 minutes in which to reconsider your decision'

It was signed by Captain Koshima as Commandant 'Japanese Field Prison' - (not I noted as Commandant of a Japanese Prisoner of War Camp).

When the interpreter read that my answer was again 'no,' he seemed genuinely upset. "No? Oh but you must say yes or they will kill you." It will be noted that he said "they" not "we." I replied with a smile, "I am sorry but I cannot do that; it would be like being Lord Haw-Haw." Clearly he had never heard of Lord Haw-Haw but walked sadly away muttering to himself.

During this testing time, I was desperately unlucky to be sick with a severe bout of a virulent type of dengue fever. I shivered and sweated alternately, running a very high temperature. I did not eat anything for several days.

When the Jap guard collected those of us who had refused the Japanese offer from our cells on the morning of 17th August, the fever had largely subsided; but I felt very weak. It did not occur to me to ask permission to be left behind because I was sick. I would not in any event have expected the Jap guard to pay any attention to such a request. But I wanted to be on parade. The treatment had been so bad since we arrived at Rangoon Jail and the outlook was so grim, that the opportunity of going out on a high note in a show of defiance of the Japanese held its attractions for me. I was fully prepared to be killed, rather than broadcast for the Japanese.

It did not turn out that way. The four of us from 'the punishment cells,' who had refused the offer, were made to stand to attention in the hot tropical sun for over an hour. In my weakened state from the fever and lack of food, and unlike the others with no hat to wear, I did not last that time. My head suddenly and quite unexpectedly went dizzy and I crashed to the ground. I was allowed to lie down in the shade until the Japs ordered us to move on when I stood up and rejoined the others.

We were marched to a compound outside the jail walls. On the way we halted to wait for the officers from the main block of solitary confinement cells. They included friends of mine from Moulmein Jail. I exchanged wry smiles with one of them, Robin Stuart from the 1/3 Gurkhas. I started surreptitiously to ask him about a mutual friend who was not with them. I was interrupted by a scream of rage. Unnoticed by me the little corporal had arrived on the scene. He went berserk and launched himself upon me, hitting my face with his open hand and fist. The beating did not last long. It was however the ferocity of the attack which stood out for all to see. The little corporal broke off hitting me and ran to a pile of wood. He selected a heavy piece. Fortunately instead of returning to hit me with it, he went to the head of our column and lead us outside the jail walls into another compound. We were stood to attention, again in the hot sun, with Burmese and Indian POW's whom many of us had commanded, facing us, the Burmese on the right and the Indians on the left. The Commandant then appeared swinging his habitual steel golf club shaft. That was all I saw before I crashed once again to the ground. On the Commandant's orders I was helped by Lieutenant Colonel Power and another officer to the wall some 20 yards or so to the rear, where I sat 'propped up' against it during the ensuing proceedings. My primary concern was to explain to the Colonel that I had been sick with a high fever for several days and that I hoped "the b........s did not think that I was afraid." Although he understood my concern and muttered a few reassuring words, he naturally had more pressing matters on his mind. He took the opportunity of having a few quick words with the other officer about the grimness of the whole situation. He indeed

68

had cause for concern, poor chap.

I had only a distant view of events. I could see what was happening but could not hear what was being said. I was of course filled in on this by others later. Colonel Power was ordered to step forward. He was then hit on the face, with open hand or closed fist, by the Burmese in turn. Some pulled their punches but others hit viciously. I saw him knocked down, get up and eventually knocked senseless. He was followed by the next senior British officer Major Nigel Loring - a very tough nut who stood up to a tremendous beating. While he was still on his feet but with his face a bloody mess, Captain Colgan, an ex-ranker regular officer in the Royal Inniskilling Fusiliers, suddenly called out "Stop this nonsense." The Commandant then made a speech, the gist of which was as follows. "I had intended to punish all of you but I have decided to allow you to reconsider your decision." On request he then allowed a brief period for discussion. Out of earshot, I could see that the beating had stopped. I could see Colonel Power struggling to his feet and addressing the officers. I was told that both he and Major Loring argued that we had to say "Yes." Otherwise the Japs would carry on indefinitely with the beatings. We could and should refuse to broadcast if it ever got to that position. Everyone agreed. We were all taken back to our cells. I was told by the interpreter that I would also be asked to say "Yes." But I never was. While my determination never to broadcast Japanese propaganda remained unshaken, as indeed was that of so many others, I would have said "Yes." 'The cherry blossoming country' was a long way off. In view of the events of the day, it was sensible for each of us to postpone his refusal to broadcast until one was actually there. This was now less likely to happen. The defiance shown to the Commandant would have revealed to him, if nothing else, that we would be extremely unreliable material as propaganda broadcasters. His face had been saved and in the end that was probably all that mattered to him.

69

The next day, the four of us from the punishment cells, who had been on parade, were moved to the main block of solitary cells. The occupants of this block had experienced a far worse time than we had in the punishment cells (apart from my two rather unlucky one-off beatings). During the hours of daylight, guards frequently patrolled the upstairs and downstairs corridors. They beat up any officer not standing rigidly to attention and bowing in a manner judged satisfactory to the guard. They also beat up Brigadier Hobson for no reason at all. The sounds of these beatings, which were usually accompanied by loud shouts, reverberated through this unhappy building. Some of them had daily endured the depressing experience of passing the cell of the dying Captain Kilgour. (See Appendix C).

But I had a piece of luck. My cell was in the middle of the upper storey overlooking the open grassy space between the solitary block and 3 Block. The officers were to spend two and a half years cultivating part of this space as a vegetable garden. From my cell I could usually hear the guard climbing up the steps and approaching along the corridor - even if he did not find anyone to shout at or discipline en route. This gave me ample time to be in position when he arrived. The one exception was a small bespectacled guard, whom we called, I am afraid rather blasphemously, 'Creeping Jesus.' He moved slowly along the corridor wearing soft shoes. Unless he had already caught someone, the first one knew of his arrival was the sight of the barrel of his rifle held at the ready. He never caught me. I was learning.

What pleased me most about the position of my cell was the view. I watched some of the BORs in 3 Block using the open space. I also spotted occasionally among them one or two of those officers who had been with me in Moulmein. Unknown to me those who had said "Yes" had been released from solitary into 3 Block the day I was moved. This was great news for me as it meant that the rest of us were likely to join them before too long.

Until then I had begun to think that the Japs would keep us in solitary indefinitely. Another indication of a changed attitude was that there were no more questionnaires to answer.

It was a joy to see the green open space, the sunshine and the sky. I watched the birds and even tried unsuccessfully to tame one of them by leaving grains of rice on the windowsill beyond the bars. Now that I no longer had to deal with Jap questionnaires I found that I could pass my time more imaginatively. 'Stone walls do not a prison make nor iron bars a cage.'

2nd September 1942 was my 21st birthday. During the morning ablutions, I mentioned this to my neighbour, Jock Ferrier of the 5th/17th Dogras who had been captured with Colonel Power at the Sittang. As soon as we were back in our cells and had heard the guard clanking down the stairs, Jock attracted my attention. He told me that he had a present for me. A bundle of Burmese Cheroots then appeared in the passage outside my cell tied to a piece of string. Smoking was forbidden. He asked me rather anxiously to let him know how many there were. If one had fallen out in the passage, it would have been unpleasant for both of us. He then learned for the first time that I did not have any matches. After he had digested this unwelcome piece of information he told me that he had no matches to spare but that I should standby again. A lighted cheroot then appeared outside my cell door tied to the same piece of string. I decided to smoke them all - one after the other. But by the time I was halfway through the second one I felt rather sick. It was not the most successful present I have ever received, but it was my only one on my 21st birthday. It was generous of Jock Ferrier, who had acquired the cheroots at some personal risk from a BOR bringing our food.

Six days later on 8th September we were all moved into 3 Block with the exception of Brigadier Hobson who joined us on 15th September. On that day Captain Koshima was replaced as Commandant.

CHAPTER XII

REFLECTIONS ON THE BROADCASTING EPISODE

Although I was unaware of this, some of the senior officers from the main solitary block were interviewed by the Commandant with his interpreter present, after they had said 'No' to the original offer. All were separate interviews and ended in blows, followed by the cessation of meals for a time. There were advantages in that time in being only a Second Lieutenant, as no subalterns were interviewed.

The ten minute ultimatum was then circulated to all. Colonel Power's interview is worth referring to as it throws some light on the character of Captain Koshima. The Colonel was misguided enough to say to the Commandant that the Japanese were an exceptionally brave race and he admired them for it, but that there were other qualities, as well as physical courage, which mattered in human beings. The dialogue then went as follows:

Captain Koshima (angrily) "What qualities?"

Colonel Power "Well, kindness for one."

Captain Koshima (in a violent rage) "Kind! Kind! I am kind. I let you live."

He then started to hit the Colonel.

Unfortunately for many months, really until we were joined by new faces with unprejudiced minds - airmen shot down etc. - the fact that some had said "Yes" before the parade on 17th August and then got early release from 'solitary' permeated through and adversely affected relations in the Officers' Barrack Room at No.3 Block. Some officers - not the two who were beaten - grossly exaggerated the episode. It was even referred to as "a blood bath." One of my friends for whom I had a great respect had said "Yes" when the 10 minute ultimatum was delivered because he assumed that everyone would. It must be remembered that in 'solitary' all communications with others were forbidden and severely punished if caught. When he saw his comrades being taken out he 'felt awful' and was vastly relieved when they were brought back. He did not enjoy the three weeks before we were all released from 'solitary.' He was also quite determined never to broadcast.

My explanation of the reason for my uncharacteristically fainting was universally accepted, as I knew it would be. [In my introduction I referred to there being occasions when perhaps I did not conduct myself quite as well as I would have wished. This was not one of them. My mental attitude throughout was defiant and unafraid. My fainting was entirely due to the physical causes which I have described]. For my part I fully accepted the explanation of my friend and others who had said "Yes" on the delivery of the 10-minute ultimatum. I must admit, however, that at the time I found it difficult to understand those who had said "Yes" immediately on receipt of that contemptible document. Nevertheless it remained true, that we all said "Yes" in the end. While some were beaten beforehand and briefly starved, only two were beaten up on the actual parade - albeit very badly and in shameful circumstances: but beatings were hardly uncommon at that time. It is however fair to say that I was certainly not the only officer who believed that he was being marched out to his death on 17th August 1942.

[After we regained our freedom Colonel Power and Major Loring tried unsuccessfully to bring Captain Koshima to justice. I attach copy of a letter on the subject written by Colonel Power to HQ Jullunder Area in India on 5th September 1945 (Appendix C)].

I quote below an extract relating to his time in solitary confinement from a poem entitled *A Lay of Rangoon Gaol* written

in pencil by Colonel Power early in his captivity and found in a
drawer of a desk in his family home after his death.

If you'll listen awhile, I'll tell you the tale
Of when I was a captive in Rangoon gaol.

Each morning, at seven, we daily parade
And empty our pails in a cesspit we've made.
Then a wash at a tap - a scrum did you say?
But we've cleaned ourselves in a sort of a way.

At nine is our breakfast - molasses and rice;
At ten there's a hunt for the pestilent lice
Once again there is rice, when one o'clock comes
And also some dahl, made of lentils - like crumbs.

My room is a cell, with a grille for a door,
There's a bar and a padlock; a concrete floor
Then my bed is a board, just six feet by two,
My bedding a blanket which is not very new.

My shirt is in rags and my vest is in holes,
My boots very soon will be minus their soles.
My shorts are incredibly dirty and worn
But at least they are whole and not woefully torn.

On each of our doors a large notice proclaims
The rank of the inmate, his age and his name.
Like a bear or a chimp in a cage at the zoo
And we also have numbers, as criminals do.

Then we probably doze for one hour or two.
When it's time to prepare our evening stew.

It's rice, a chapatti and a watery mess -
Oh! I wonder what's given to Rudolph Hess.

To talk is forbidden, no smoking's allowed,
We don't see the sun, we live under a cloud
And I feel that to live in a solitary cell
Must closely resemble one aspect of Hell.

Colonel Power summed up life in 'solitary' in another delightful piece of light verse:

> I am monarch of fourteen by eight,
> the extent of my solitary house.
> From the centre all round to the gate
> I am lord of the cockroach and louse.

My final reflection on the Broadcasting Episode is this. It is my considered opinion that the Japanese should be ashamed of the conduct of Captain Koshima. In particular to arrange for two senior officers, whose only crime was that they did not choose to betray their country, to be beaten until they were knocked senseless by or in the presence of troops they had commanded, was despicable. It was yet one more example of the unchivalrous and brutal behaviour of the Imperial Japanese Army towards its prisoners of war.

CHAPTER XII

LIFE IN RANGOON JAIL

8th September 1942 - 25th April 1945

Our release from solitary and the departure of Captain Koshima in September 1942 marked a watershed in the treatment of myself and my comrades. We were never subjected again to such ill-treatment as I have described. This does not mean that there were no more beatings. There were. But they were mostly, although by no means entirely, by way of reprimand where the guards genuinely believed that the rules had been broken rather than the vicious, unprovoked assaults of the previous few months. We grew accustomed to these and they did not mean a great deal.

Life in Rangoon Jail settled down into a routine, which while it had its problems, some severe as I shall recount, was one to which the majority of us were able to adjust. This period ended on 25th April 1945. On that date all British and American prisoners of war, except for those seriously ill, were marched out of the jail.

[I must make it clear however that my account of life in Rangoon Jail during this period is limited to the personal experiences of myself and my comrades. In particular it does not relate to the treatment of airmen shot down in 1944 and 1945. On the instructions of the Japanese High Command they were treated as war criminals for alleged acts of indiscriminate bombing. They were subjected to lengthy spells in solitary confinement followed by a poor diet and lack of medical attention in the strictly segregated 8 Block].

I have decided to cover the whole of this period in one chapter, dividing up the different aspects of life in separate sections.

PLAN OF RANGOON JAIL
PREPARED BY ELEANOR AND IMOGEN DE GALLEANI
FROM AN AERIAL PHOTOGRAPH.

In most cases I have tried to illustrate such aspects with anecdotes describing specific events.

I set out below a list of the sections:

A   Description of prison and inmates of Blocks.

B   Description of the routine in 3 Block.

C   Brief details of some of the officers senior to me in 3 Block at the time of our release from solitary Confinement.

D   The possibilities of escape.

E   Air raids on the Jail.

F   Work parties in and out of the Jail.

      1.   Officers work in the jail

      2.   Work parties out of the jail

G.   Health

      1.   The prisoners generally

      2.   My own health record

H.   Our attitude to Japanese discipline.

I.   Leisure activities

A.   Description of prison and inmates of blocks

Rangoon Central Jail was a jail purpose-built by the British, but had not in fact been used as such for several years before the war. It was in a filthy condition. The main buildings were seven blocks radiating from a central water tower like the spokes of a wheel. The lay-out can be worked out by studying the photograph of the jail taken from the air and the plan on which the various buildings are numbered. I set out below a key to the numbers with a description of the use to which each building was put.

1.   Number 1 Block - Chinese

2.   Number 2 Block - Indians and Gurkhas

3.   Number 3 Block

All the prisoners taken by the Japanese in the retreat from Burma in 1942 were placed in this block. Most were army, but there were a few US, Commonwealth and RAF airmen.

In November 1942 we were joined by a party of civilians from the recently-captured Andaman Islands. They were headed by Mr Waterfall CIE ICS the Governor. (He was knighted after the war). All civilians left Rangoon Jail on 15th April 1943 for Tavoy in South Burma.

Until June 1943, when 6 Block was opened, shot-down airmen and the few army prisoners captured after the retreat from Burma were placed in 3 Block.

On 10th May 1944 all US and British Commonwealth prisoners in 3 Block were moved to 6 Block in exchange for a number of the army prisoners in 6 Block, most of whom had been captured from Wingate's first Chindit expedition.

4.   Number 4 Block

This comprised the Punishment Block (as named by the British) where I spent most of my time in 'solitary' (see Chapter X) and another small building used for storage. After our removal to the main solitary block on 18th August 1942, these buildings were never occupied by prisoners so far as I am aware.

5.   Number 5 Block

The main solitary confinement block, containing two storeys of cells each approximately fourteen feet by eight feet.

6.   Number 6 Block

Opened in June 1943 to take allied airmen and army

prisoners from Wingate's first Chindit expedition. In December 1943 Major Loring was ordered by the Japs to take command of this block. He brought with him Captain Henstock as his second in command.

As stated above, on 10th May 1944 there was an exchange between the US and the British Commonwealth prisoners in 3 Block and the majority of the British army Chindit prisoners in 6 Block. [At the time this was sad for me as we lost two New Zealand fighter-pilots and two US Airforce officers, all of whom I knew well, in addition to three or four outstanding Australian non-commissioned aircrew]. Major Loring with Captain Henstock remained in command of 6 Block.

6a.   From June 1943 this was the prison hospital to which I was moved in early 1944 as subsequently related.

7.   Number 7 Block - Indians

8.   Number 8 Block

For three months from November 1942 this was occupied by Dutch prisoners. They were in poor condition and pretty demoralised on arrival. We had only occasional surreptitious contact with them, but we observed their failure to keep their compound clean. About 260 of them died while they were with us. They departed in January 1943 for an unknown destination, which according to rumour was Moulmein.

In 1944 and 1945 it was used exclusively for Allied aircrew and strictly segregated.

9.   The central Water Tower

This was used as a Japanese store and as a drawing point for water. It contained a deep well used whenever the water supply failed. It also contained a side passage which Colonel Mackenzie used as his operating theatre.

10.   The Main Entrance, the Commandant's Office and
        the Guardroom.

Blocks 1, 2, 3, 6, 7 and 8 each in its own compound had five large rooms upstairs and five down. A corridor ran the whole length of the block on each storey and was separated from the rooms by wooden bars; on the opposite side of the room there were five windows with iron bars but no glass. In the compound of each block there was a latrine shed and a large trough of water. A lean-to cookhouse was built against a wall of each compound. At the end of the compound facing the central water tower there were iron railings so that the sentry could walk round the water tower and see what was happening in any compound.

B.   Description of the routine in 3 Block

On our release from solitary the officers occupied the two upstairs rooms nearest the central tower. The downstairs room at the far end was used as a hospital. [However, as stated above from December 1943 the main hospital for the prisoners in both 3 and 6 Block was in 6 Block]. The rest of the rooms in the block were occupied by the BORs. The men from each regiment (i.e. West Yorkshire, The Duke of Wellington's Regiment (The Dukes), The King's Own Yorkshire Light Infantry (KOYLI), The Inniskilling Fusiliers, The Gloucesters and The Cameronians) kept together.

'Tenko' (Japanese for 'roll call') took place at 8.30am and 8.00pm. We had to use Tokyo time. By local sun time it would have been 6.00am and 5.30pm (ie 2 ½ hours earlier). We had to dress in shirts and shorts and fall in by rooms. The officers paraded facing the water tower. When the Jap guard appeared the senior British officer shouted 'Kiotsuke' ('Come to attention')

81

and then 'Bango' (number), we then shouted out our numbers in Japanese. "Ichi, nee, san, she, go, roko etc...." [We were told that when there were only a few BORs in 3 Block at the beginning they numbered in English. Apparently there were thirteen of them and they shouted out:

"One, two, three, four, five, six, seven, eight, nine, ten, jack, queen, king"] The next order was 'keri' ('salute') and we all gave a mass bow which was acknowledged by the Guard Commander with a salute. We then fell out for breakfast. The officers' work in the garden started at 10.00am and the men's work parties usually set out at that time. (See below)

As an officer and one of the early arrivals I was given an iron bedstead, which was less uncomfortable than a wooden bed, as there were gaps for my hips. I was also issued with a mosquito net, which was a great boon. There was fortunately no malaria in Rangoon, but I had already suffered from dengue fever both in Moulmein and in 'solitary.' In neither case did I have a mosquito net. Moreover the mosquitos at certain times of the year were a torment at night for those without mosquito nets. Additionally I brought with me from 'solitary' an old army great coat and a blanket.

The bush shirt and shorts in which I was captured became more and more tattered, despite efforts at patching. But we only had to wear our clothes at 'tenko' or when taking out work parties. The rest of the time we all went around in very brief loin cloths. As I have mentioned, I went bare foot after my second beating in solitary.

Except when the water supply broke down, when we had to draw an inadequate supply from the well, we always used the trough in the compound to wash ourselves. We did this by splashing water from our mess tins over us. We younger officers were fascinated by some of the descriptive tattoos on the lower regions of the bodies of a few regular soldiers. I certainly do not intend to describe them, but I often wondered what their wives or partners

82

made of them.

Like every other prisoner, I was obsessed with the subject of food as a topic of conversation. The reason was simple. The diet was inadequate and there was not enough of what there was. However, my memory so retentive in matters concerned with people, both prisoners and Japs, and for events, lets me down over details of what we ate and how it was cooked. I cannot remember for instance all the details of 'the great liver controversy,' 'the January rice riots,' 'tomato Tuesday' and even why we called one of the civilians from the Andaman Islands 'Mango Kemp.' This was despite the fact that I was the originator of at least one of the titles. In any event, even if I did remember the full stories I would not recount in my Memories. Suffice to say that there were instances of human greed in 3 Block - and that unfortunately is an understatement. To be honest, however, I do remember that when it was my turn to dish out a meal how tempting it was to make sure that my mess tin contained at least as many goodies from the stew (e.g. the odd piece of meat) as anyone else. I also remember what a deterrent it was to have numerous pairs of eyes silently watching my every action.

In order to supply the accurate information which many of my readers would like, I have delved into my sources.

All the cooking was done by our own men with home-made brick fireplaces (sometimes flooded in the monsoon). The firewood ration was inadequate - about 1/3 of the British army rate. We had to cut out meals on several occasions and would have been reduced regularly from three to two per day had we not increased the firewood by burning some stairs, rafters and other pieces of wood from the building. Our rations fluctuated over the years. After October 1942, the pre-Japanese invasion stocks had run out. Our staple diet from then became rice and vegetables. The latter varied with the seasons, but overall the most common were marrow, sweet potatoes, beans, pumpkins, brinjals

83

(aubergine), cucumbers and in 3 Block the local spinach grown in the officers' garden as I shall relate. Additionally on occasions there were issues of dhal, a kind of lentil, and gram, a very hard kind of pea usually given to horses or mules. Meat, usually beef but occasionally pork, was very irregular.

In August 1943, which was a bad time of the year for vegetables but a good period for the meat ration, which had been and would in the future become much less, Bruce Toothill wrote in his diary:

'Polished rice has lost most of its vitamin content and as it is usually sold this way the Nips have devised a type of bran, made from the rice husk, which is said to contain the removed vitamin. This bran we attempt to make into a kind of porridge and serve a few spoonfuls to each man; it is palatable with salt or sugar, provided you hold your nose. It is usually dark at breakfast time, so we don't see the maggots in it!'[7]

Lunch is again rice, with perhaps a type of cabbage-water soup, made with potato tops or any green vegetable to help it down.

Dinner is usually rice and stew made of perhaps 3lbs of meat (for 40)[8] cucumbers, marrows or pumpkins - the usual selection of vegetables at this time of year. Potatoes are rare, even yams are unobtainable. Carrots are available but never reach us. Turnips are not grown in the East. Tea is served at each meal without milk or sugar; for months we just drank boiled water. There is a sugar ration of about half an ounce a day. Most people save this to sprinkle on rice when they simply cannot get it down with other things.

The above represents the basic menu.'

In addition to the rations issued by the Japs, we were able to buy a few extras. The officers received pay which was supposed to be the same as an equivalent rank in the Japanese army. However there were deductions for 'messing' and also for payment into the

'Greater East Asia Co-prosperity Sphere Savings Bank'! My pay of course remained the equivalent to a Japanese Second Lieutenant. The Japs were as unaware as I was of my promotion to Lieutenant on 1st October 1942. We also gave half of what we received into a fund for buying extras to improve the food, primarily for the sick but also for all the rest. Nevertheless there was some left and in the early days it was well worth having. I was able to buy at an exorbitant cost of course eggs (my top priority; and it is worth recording that at the time Bruce Toothill as a Captain could purchase an egg a day which he considered saved his life), soap (early on), bananas and tomatoes sometimes and also the occasional cigar, which I would pay some skilled BOR to make into cigarettes (more on this subject later). But inflation set in. Eggs became out of range of a Second Lieutenant's pay. In fact by 1945 the officers' pay and the working parties earnings were all pooled and used to buy meat and extra food for all.

C.   Details of some British officers in Rangoon Jail

In order to reduce the number of footnotes, I set out below brief details of some of the officers senior to me in 3 Block at the time of our release from 'solitary' in September 1942 and with whom I came into contact in a subordinate position during my captivity. I also describe my relations with them. I would emphasise that these remarks are purely personal, in a personal memoir, and are not intended to be a balanced assessment of the character of any of them. For instance they all shared one attribute which I have purposely not mentioned. They were all brave men. Perhaps more than one were exceptionally courageous; but it would be invidious to select individuals. However I have no intention of writing either eulogies or inoffensively and blandly about my fellow prisoners. I do not want to bore my readers.

Brigadier Clive Hobson: A business man, I believe an

85

executive in a large tobacco company trading in China. When he joined the Army he was at once promoted to Captain. This was on account of his proficiency in the Chinese language. As he had to deal with Chinese generals, it was subsequently decided to promote him to Brigadier. A tall, well-built man, he had the necessary presence.

He had an extremely difficult job as senior British officer, made much more difficult by his total lack of any Army experience. Moreover he suffered the disadvantage of starting his job immediately after enduring a terrible time in 'solitary' (see Appendix C). He did his best and improved significantly as the months went by. He conducted himself admirably during the march out of Rangoon Jail in April 1945. It was tragic that he should be killed by our own aircraft soon after giving us the wonderful news that we were free.

Colonel K P Mackenzie RAMC: He was the director of Medical Services to the 17th Indian Division and was taken prisoner with his deputy Major McCleod when the Sittang bridge was blown up.

He was a self-opinionated, very determined Scot, 51 years old when captured. When Major McCleod was unable to continue as Doctor in charge of 3 Block due to failing eyesight, Colonel Mackenzie agreed to take over. He performed this extremely difficult task, with ability and considerable organisational skill.

Early on, before he undertook any responsibility, we formed a mutual dislike. He considered I did not pay him the respect due to his rank. Unfortunately that is probably true and I made no attempt to conceal my feelings. We had six Scottish officers with us in Rangoon in September 1942. I got on extremely well with the other five. It would have been sensible for me to have made an effort to do the same with the sixth, who was in more of a position to affect my welfare than all the other five put together. But I was not always sensible in those days. However, it is perhaps worth

86

recording that at the first reunion referred to below, as one of the organisers I sat next to Colonel Mackenzie. We thoroughly enjoyed each others company.

Lieutenant Colonel (subsequently Colonel) H R Power: He had been Commanding Officer of the 5th/17th Dogra Regiment which we had expected to come to our assistance at the Battle of Pa-an. He was another taken prisoner when the Sittang bridge was blown up. After Brigadier Hobson he was the senior combatant British officer during our captivity. An intelligent, civilised man, possessed of infinite tact, he was universally liked and respected.

It is pleasant to state that from the beginning I always got on extremely well with him. We kept in touch after the War; we used occasionally to meet at Lord's to watch a Test Match and on one occasion attended the 17th Indian Division reunion dinner together. A number of years after our release the Colonel and I, together with Captain Willy Wilding, who had been captured in 1943 with Wingate's first Chindit expedition and Captain John Harvey, who was one of the few taken prisoner in 1944, organised a reunion dinner of ex-Rangoon officers at a London club. This was repeated for the next two years. We succeeded in attracting quite a large percentage and I personally found it fascinating to meet them again. Sadly the Colonel died after the third reunion and that was the end of that.

Major Nigel Loring: He was an able, dashing regular soldier in his middle thirties, seconded from a smart Indian cavalry regiment, the name of which I forget, to command a small unit of the Burma Frontier Force. Rumour had it that he had blotted his copy book. Too much drink? Another officer's wife? We never knew. It may not be true anyway.

I have already recounted how well he stood up to the tremendous beating by the Burmese soldiers at the Broadcasting parade. He was selected by the Commandant to take over command of No.6 Block in December 1943.

87

He was a strong personality with a tendency to bully junior officers. Soon after we came out of 'solitary' we clashed. He picked on me and remarked that the sooner the Army got rid of me after the War the better. I replied: "If all senior officers are as selfish as you and Colonel MacKenzie I wouldn't touch it with a barge pole." I had a specific, but on subsequent reflection unjustified, reason for my charge of selfishness; but it is irrelevant to the point I am making. I thought he was going to hit me. He just controlled himself. The next day, on advice, I apologised for being rude, at the same time making it clear that I had no intention of being pushed around. This nearly caused another row. But he accepted my apology - just. I have regretted many of my outspoken comments of those days; but not that one. He never picked on me again. I felt that I had enough to cope with without allowing myself to be bullied by senior officers.

Nevertheless he was a leader and I would willingly have followed him in battle.

Captain Tiny Henstock of the 2nd/7th Rajput Regiment: A huge man of some six foot six in his early thirties, he had been a tea planter in Ceylon before the War.

After we came out of 'solitary,' he was appointed to command the platoon of prisoners from the West Yorkshire Regiment. I was appointed his second-in-command.

When Major Loring took over 6 Block in December 1943 at the request of the Commandant, he persuaded Tiny Henstock to accompany him as his second-in-command and righthand man.

Another strong personality and extremely outspoken, Tiny Henstock was not universally popular, particularly in 6 Block. He could, however, be very amusing and we always remained good friends. As I shall recount he did me a great service when I was sent over to the hospital in 6 Block.

I liked the idea of becoming a tea planter in Ceylon after the War. He encouraged this and promised, with the help of his brother who had an important position in the tea industry, to do what he could. But after the War he wrote to say that while he could get me a job he advised against it. Ceylon was on the way to independence as Sri Lanka and he considered that there was no future for British tea planters. In any event at that time I was reading Law at Cambridge. I have never had any doubt that I was better suited to being a solicitor in London than a tea planter in Ceylon.

Captain Bunny Bunten of the Cameronians: He was a regular Army officer and I believe a fine Rugby Union centre three-quarter who had played for the Army and obtained a trial cap for Scotland.

The first time I saw him, apart from the Broadcasting parade on 17th August, he behaved typically. We were standing by our beds in the officers' room in 3 Block, having just been brought out of 'solitary.' We were being inspected by the Little Corporal, who shouted at Bunny: "You are English." He replied: "No I am not." And then after a pause: "I am Scottish." The Little Corporal, of all people, was hardly likely to understand such political niceties - and we all thought we were going to be sent back to 'solitary.'

Fiercely loyal to his Cameronian troops, who were not universally popular among the officers, and to Scotland, he came in for a lot of badinage from me amongst others. He took all this with great good nature.

I shall be recounting the episode when I was his second-in-command of a work party leaving the docks just as our bombers appeared on the scene.

D.   The possibilities of escape

Not long after our release from solitary confinement, the Japs ordered all the officers to give their word of honour not to try to escape. Each officer was told to sign a piece of paper which read as follows: 'I, the undersigned, solemnly swear on my honour

89

that I will not, under any circumstances, attempt escape.'

I have previously referred to the duty of a prisoner of war to try to escape. For this reason it was decided to hold a meeting in order to give each officer the opportunity to express his views.

My opinion was that any promise not to escape given under duress was null and void and need not be kept. We were under duress. Our treatment since our arrival in Rangoon Jail, culminating in the broadcasting episode demonstrated clearly that the Japs would force us to sign in the end. There was near unanimity among us that there was no point in refusing. I can only remember one speaker, Captain Bunny Bunten of the Cameronians, advocating refusal.

[Interestingly, however, a week or so earlier about 18,000 British and Australian prisoners in Changi Jail in Singapore had faced the same decision. Initially only four prisoners signed the piece of paper. Three days later in Selerang, to where they had been marched by the Japs, all the rest signed. Up to that time, their treatment had born no comparison to ours in Rangoon Jail. The ruthless reaction of the Jap Commandant to the initial defiance of the Singapore prisoners changed that. It was a watershed. It led to the cruelties of the Moulmein - Bangkok railway].[9]

As the officers filed up the compound to sign the pieces of paper on the tables at the end, a mocking voice called out from among the watching BORs.

"You are signing your honour away, gentlemen!"
I did not look on it like that. If I had decided to attempt to escape, I would not have given a second thought to the fact that I had given my word of honour not to attempt escape in view of the circumstances under which it had been given. I did not however believe that the possibility of escape would ever arise. But here I was wrong.

My main reason for believing that I would never even contemplate the possibility of escape was this. It was generally accepted that no white man who succeeded in escaping from Rangoon Jail or from a work party, neither of which would have been too difficult, would have had any chance of avoiding detection for long in an Asiatic country, such as Burma. Moreover, the Burmese were hostile towards the British. A white escapee would not have a 'cat in hell's chance' of travelling the length of Burma. [This should not have been the case with Indians. But in fact the only escape of Indian POW's that I know of was from a Japanese work camp in China. A mixed party of thirteen (including all four VCO's captured at Pa-an[10)] escaped into an area controlled by the Chinese Army. From there they were flown back to India].

There was also another factor. The Japanese did not behave towards their prisoners of war in the same way as did the Germans and Italians. An escape would have serious consequences on those remaining. It would not just mean a loss of privileges, as in German and Italian POW camps. There were in any event no privileges to lose. A recaptured escapee would face severe physical punishment, if not death, and not just a week or two in the 'cooler' (POW slang for solitary confinement in German POW camps).

However, as I shall relate in Chapter XIII (The March) the situation was different on 28th April 1945.

E.   Air raids on the Jail

It was only after our release from 'Solitary' which coincided with the end of the monsoon in September 1942 that we saw for the first time any allied aircraft and they came over only occasionally either singularly or in pairs. Nevertheless they boosted our morale.

On 24th December 1942, we heard bombs dropped for the first time. This was a raid on Rangoon by a single aircraft. It dropped its bombs on the road outside the guardhouse, killing or wounding all the guard who were lined up in the entrance following a change-over. Unfortunately most of the unpleasant ones were in the guard which had just been relieved. But this was more than made up by the news that the 'Little Corporal' had been killed outright in his office. He was a sadistic little swine who had carried out with enthusiasm the orders of Captain Koshima to ill-treat the prisoners and indeed had frequently exceeded those orders. We were all delighted that he had been killed. It would be hypocritical to pretend otherwise.

There was of course a reaction on the part of the Japanese. We had no more food that day. In fact it was not until the afternoon of the following day that the cooks were sent for to collect the rations. There were no special 'goodies' for us on Christmas Day 1942 as there were on subsequent Christmas Days.

Air raids increased during the early months of 1943; but it was not until the monsoon started to peter out that the aircraft came over in considerable numbers. The Jail was only 600 yards from the docks and was also quite close to the railway station as well as several local Japanese headquarters. It was however conspicuous from the air and we had been told by recently shot-down airmen that it was known to be occupied by allied prisoners of war. After some adjacent bombs had fallen during one raid, we dug slit trenches covering them with corrugated iron sheets. But I for one did not bother occupying them - that is until after 28th November 1943, when the following incident took place:

That afternoon I was playing bridge in a four which included Brigadier Hobson and Major Loring.

There was the sound of planes. Several officers ran into the corridor. They reported that there were some 25 'Liberators' flying towards us. We assumed that they were intending to bomb the docks - some 600 yards away. We decided to continue with our game. The bidding was brisk; but there was tenseness in our voices. We were waiting for the bombs to fall. They came with a resounding crash shaking our building violently. There was relief in Nigel Loring's voice as he called "6 spades." That was to be the last bid. There was the short screech of further bombs right on top of us followed by deafening explosions on either side of our building.

Our cards flew in all directions. "God-dammit" exclaimed Nigel Loring, as he picked himself up. "The best bridge hand I ever had."

I was the possessor of a metal helmet - a quite useless object which I had somehow acquired. As soon as the building had stopped shaking and I could see my way through the cloud of dust, I 'plonked' this on my head and announced to all and sundry:

"I am now going to inspect the compound in my capacity as an air raid warden."

The laughter which greeted my antics was suddenly stilled. Private Bull, breathless from running up the outside steps, appeared in the corridor. He announced through the wooden railings:

"Sergeant Major 'erd is dead round the back."

A few seconds later I heard him repeating the same doleful words to the next Barrack Room.

CSM Joe Herd of 'The Dukes' had lived in the officers' room as did the other Warrant officers. He was one of two killed in our block. In addition, two were seriously wounded and a number suffered minor injuries.

A stick of four bombs, apparently of 500lbs each, had fallen in the Jail, from a plane which had lagged behind the others. One had landed harmlessly, the second in No.2 Compound killing 22 Indians and injuring a further 36 and the third and fourth in our compound on either side of the building. 'Tail-end Charlie' had left his mark.

When the sound of a single plane was heard on the following night the 29th November we all moved at once to the slit trenches. Unbelievably the plane dropped its bombs in the Jail and one fell in our compound. Tragically some American airmen had dug their trench much deeper than the rest of us. This was a mistake. A bomb landed near and they were buried deep. Despite frantic efforts from their comrades most of them died. One of them had boasted that with the new American bombsight they could drop a bomb in a bucket from 20,000 feet. Despite this claim we had always been quietly amused to notice that the American airmen were always the first to reach their slit trench when the sound of planes was heard. But this cruel retribution was not amusing.

There were many further and bigger air raids, but the Jail was never hit again. Nevertheless our confidence in the skill and accuracy of allied bombing had been dented. This lack of confidence was not improved so far as I was concerned when a friendly American airman described what took place when their planes reached the target area. "Come on, come on. Bombs away chaps. Let's get the hell out of here and back to Cal (Calcutta)."

As I shall describe in the following section, work parties were sent repeatedly to target areas.

There is no doubt that allied bombing increased the stress of living in Rangoon Jail. While conditions in the Jail after our release from 'solitary' were not as bad as in many other camps (e.g. on the railway in Thailand and Malaya or in Java), few other Japanese prison camps had to endure this particular stressful feature. However it must be stated that this aspect of life was far worse for the other ranks than for the officers. They went out on work parties daily, whereas the officers (due to the number of Indian Army and RAF officers) perhaps once a week at most.

F.   Work parties

1. Officers' work in the jail

From the date of our release from 'solitary,' it was the duty of the officers to cultivate the garden which formed the greater part of the large grass compound between 3 Block and the solitary Block. This green area of perhaps four or five acres, containing a number of trees providing welcome shade at times, was an inestimable benefit not available to the other blocks. I have already described what a pleasure it was for me in my last few weeks of 'solitary' to look over this oasis in the arid prison.

Of course we were subject all the time to the supervision and instructions of the Japanese. They were always impatient for quick results; and were far less knowledgeable about agriculture than several of our officers (tea planters for instance). I am more concerned with describing what it was like to work in the garden over the years than with what we actually grew or how successful it was. Nevertheless as the reader may be interested I have referred to Colonel Power's diary and am indebted to him for some of the details included below.

Amongst other vegetables we grew Japanese radishes (very dreary) in abundance, local spinach (excellent), cucumbers, brinjals (aubergines), sweet potatoes and carrots. We used illegally to eat some of our carrots raw. Knowledgeable chaps said that they contained vitamin A and were good for the eyesight.

Bill Cayley (of 7 Baluch), who had been a tea planter in India, had the bright idea of growing corn cobs. They grew high and provided both shade for one or two of us and more important privacy from the Jap guards as we weeded inside the two rows. We were not allowed to keep any of the cobs and eventually were forbidden to grow any more. The guards disliked our not being in full view all the time.

At times the work was hard (e.g. breaking hard ground with inadequate garden tools) or unpleasant (e.g. raking our excreta collected from the benjo shed into the vegetable beds as manure). Usually the work was not strenuous but strenuous enough on an inadequate diet. It consisted of weeding, watering and cultivating the top soil. We dug the beds after the crops had been harvested. The hours were not long. For the most part it was not an unpleasant way of passing the time - and I remember many long and enjoyable conversations.

For a long time we were fortunate to have a guard in charge of us with whom we established a friendly relationship - at least when he was out of sight of his superiors. He was extremely amusing and a natural mimic. His name was Kume. We called him 'Kume San.' He referred to himself as "Meestak me." We eventually worked this one out. He was quite prepared to discuss his superiors. During one 'Yasmi' (Jail Nip for 'rest period'). He gave us his views on the rival merits of Captain Koshima and his successor Lieutenant Sakimota. "English officers no like Koshima. He put them in cells. Ho, ho, ho. Me think Koshima very good man, Sakimota no good." He then explained why. After breakfast he and his comrades when they went to wash their dishes had to pass the officers' 'benjo.' They always gave the enthroned Commandant a smart eyes right and salute. Koshima always returned the salute equally smartly, whereas Sakimota just glared at them.[11]
Inevitably there were occasions when we had an unpleasant guard in charge; but we did not let that worry us much.

It was only during the monsoon season of 1944 that the officers were put on harder work, such as demolishing a building, carrying bricks and building a wall, moving girders and sacks of rice. Only once during our captivity did we leave the jail as an officers' work party. This was on a memorable occasion, again in 1944, when the local inhabitants of Rangoon were edified by the spectacle of British officers dressed only with the briefest of loin cloths pushing cart loads of manure through the streets. Philip Stibbe writes:

"We amused ourselves by imagining what the reaction of the Poona Club would have been if they could have seen us!"

2.   Work parties out of the jail

From the beginning work parties of BORs were sent out in Rangoon. After we came out of 'solitary' they were always accompanied by an officer. We dressed in shirts and shorts (increasingly tattered as time went by). The officer would shout out commands in Japanese as we carried out the ceremonial drill going in and out of the Jail.

At first the work was usually easy and the work parties visited pleasant locations in Rangoon, such as former European Clubs. From these the men would come back with concealed books and other goodies. [The books were a source of contention between voracious readers like me and habitual smokers who wanted the paper to make cigarettes from the cheroots which could be purchased. I remember a hard won victory over the fate of the greater part of a magnificent set of Charles Dickens novels, the paper from which apparently made excellent cigarettes]. As most of the officers were from the Indian Army and allowed no contact with any Indian troops, there were a disproportionate number of us. It was at first decided that no officer under the rank of Captain should accompany work parties. We Second Lieutenants considered this unfair and said so. We were stuck all the time in the dreary precincts of the jail and missed the stimulus of travelling through the city - well worth the price of an occasional face slapping by an impatient guard in charge. As soon as allied bombing increased and work parties started to go to target areas, the attitude of the Captains changed. We must all share the same risks! Such was human nature in Rangoon Jail.

As it happens, no work party was actually bombed. We were usually sent to clear up the mess the day after a bombing raid. For instance on one occasion on arrival at the station the British officer was told: "English drop bombs. English take away." They then had to dig up an unexploded bomb, load it onto the back of a lorry and sit on it during a bumpy journey to the outskirts of Rangoon. It exploded when they were just out of range on the way back. I remember discussing the episode with the officer in charge - I believe he was Hugh Mercer of 7 Baluch but I am not certain of this. He said they had great difficulty keeping the bomb still, despite the use of a rope and sitting on it. They sang military songs to keep up their spirits. I asked how the Jap guards behaved. He replied that they were as scared as our party and joined in the celebration when they heard the bomb going up just after our lorry had left.

For many months the work parties were engaged in digging an air raid shelter for the Japanese Headquarters in Rangoon in the grounds of the Nyoma School. First a huge hole was dug and then many more months were spent in piling a large mound of earth on top of the shelter. The men were treated like slave labour; the hours became longer and longer. The guard in charge was a huge powerful man who used his strength when beating our men which he did frequently. He was nicknamed 'The Bulldozer.' We usually had more than one officer on this particular work party. I went more than once and did not enjoy the experience.

As the air raids increased the coolies left the city. Our work parties were sent to take their place throughout the city but particularly in the docks which was a target area. We would unload barges, usually carrying sacks of rice and sometimes even larger ships. On one occasion I was second-in-command of a large work party under Captain Bunny Bunten. We had just left the docks and were marching together ahead of the work party towards the Jail. The air raid sirens sounded. Soon anti-aircraft guns went into action. Captain Bunten took charge. He asked me to lead on at the same pace, while he went to the rear. "We will show these .... how British troops behave." He said. I continued to march towards the Jail. Soon the planes were overhead. I saw their silver shapes intermingled with puffs of smoke as anti-aircraft shells exploded. It was with satisfaction that I saw the Jap guards run for cover. None of our men fell out but I heard a shout from behind me "Get a ...... move on."

As I led the march across the road to the entrance of the

jail, a man behind me said:

"We are all right now. If they drop their bombs, they will land well in front of us."

As he spoke the bombs started to fall. They landed behind us.

A friend of mine on reading the above account in Appendix E of Part 1, wrote to me criticising the orders issued by Captain Bunten. I disagreed. As he (Captain Bunten) explained to me afterwards:

"I could not have our chaps breaking ranks and running for cover all over Rangoon."

He was right. It was essential that the Japanese, contemptuous of us anyway for being prisoners, should not be given any reason to despise us further. His was one of the few examples of firm leadership I was to meet during my captivity and I responded gladly.

Despite the constant danger of air raids, there were a number of work parties which I did enjoy. It was fascinating being driven in a lorry through the streets of Rangoon and observing the activities of free men and women. Moreover there was always the Schwedagon Pagoda, in all its golden beauty particularly in the early morning and evening sunshine, dominating every scene.

It was the task of the officer to interpret the orders of the guard in charge, spoken of course in Japanese, and pass these on to the men. Mostly the guards in charge were reasonable and more friendly than those in the Jail; (the 'Bulldozer' was a one-off) but others sometimes would give the officer the occasional face-slapping, particularly if he argued that the task demanded of the men was too onerous. But it was stimulating and at times challenging. I believed it was good for me to take out work parties. (Except of course to target areas and to the Bulldozer's domain).

One work party early in 1945 is worth recording. I was in charge of a small party which embarked from the docks on a motor boat. I cannot remember how far we went or what work we did. But on the way back, the Jap guard said we could have a swim if we wanted to. I was one of those who immediately stripped off their clothes and dived in, without a thought about pollution. Many years later in January 1996 from a cruise boat *The Caledonian Star* I looked down on the filthy water in Rangoon harbour. I thought we must have been mad to have swum in it. I became ill with jaundice shortly after my swim and still believe that the swim was the cause of it.

G.   Health

1.   The prisoners generally

The Japanese record in looking after the health of the prisoners in Rangoon Jail was appalling. Over 35% of those captured in 1942 died. The death rate of Wingate's first Chindits captured in 1943 was 60%; but I believe this included some who did not reach Rangoon and many of those who did were in poor condition.

The biggest killer was Beri-Beri, caused by a deficiency of vitamin B. I have already referred to the unpleasant rice/bran gruel, which was our only source of vitamin B. This disease took two forms. The victim either developed chronic diarrhoea and grew thinner and thinner until he became only skin and bones or he swelled up to an enormous size, starting with his legs. Both were fatal. Beri-Beri and some of the other diseases to which I will refer later could have been prevented or cured by medicines and a better diet. These were not forthcoming.

It is perhaps fair to say that the percentage of deaths was a little higher than it need have been. Some found the conditions too much for them and on becoming ill there were those who turned their faces to the wall and died. There is evidence to support this contention in the fact that none of my fellow officer prisoners died. This record was shared by Captain Bunten's Cameronians who were all with us at the end - despite most of them having spent their childhoods in deprived areas of Glasgow. But they were exceptionally tough.

There was one terrible case which I have to relate. Fortunately it was a one-off. The crew of an American bomber shot down near Rangoon in 1944 were brought into the solitary cells of No.5 Block. With one exception they were all badly burnt. For several days they were left by the Japs with their wounds undressed. When our medics were allowed to treat their burns, it was too late. In some cases their faces and other parts of their bodies were a mass of maggots. With the one exception they all died screaming in agony as they had done since their arrival. The Japs supplied no painkillers. We could hear the screams at night and even more so during the day as we worked in the garden below the solitary block. It was, I believe, an Anglican bishop captured at Singapore who said "We can forgive but we cannot forget."

When we came out of 'solitary' in September 1942 Major MacLeod (the Deputy Director of Medical Services under Colonel Mackenzie to the 17th Indian Division) took charge of the doctoring. Soon afterwards he was joined by two Indian doctors from the Andaman Islands' party. But these Indian doctors found it discouraging to work without drugs and dressings and with patients whose diets they were unable to improve. They left with the other civilians in April 1943. Bruce Toothill wrote '... from them we obtained a stethoscope and thermometer, so we had a better opportunity of finding out what was wrong with the sick man, though we could do little about it afterwards.'

At about that time Major MacLeod, whose eyesight was failing, handed over to Colonel Mackenzie. Whether or not he was a better doctor, I do not know, but he was certainly much more effective. He organised his medical staff and orderlies properly. He also emphasised to the rest of us the importance of hygiene.

In January 1944, as I have related, the hospital in 6 Block was established for all the white POWs (except for those in solitary and 8 Block). Major Raymond Ramsay, on his release from solitary at the end of 1943, took over command of the hospital. He had been the Brigade Medical Officer to Brigadier Wingate's first Chindit expedition. With almost total lack of any medicines, medical equipment or other medical facilities, he had to cope with Beri-Beri, dysentery, jungle sores (very prevalent among the Chindits), malaria, an outbreak of cholera and many other diseases. His performance in the jail was quite remarkable. He was awarded an MBE. I was not alone in thinking that he deserved a higher award. After his death on 3 April 1997 The Times had a four-column obituary (including a photograph) covering his work in Rangoon Jail and his career as a surgeon after it. I quote a short extract as it gives some idea how he coped with the lack of drugs and medical facilities:

'He proved an inventive pharmacologist. Men from the work-parties found what they called 'Blue Stones' - copper sulphate - which were crushed and mixed with water as an antidote for jungle sores. Guards were also bribed to bring in poppies which were fermented to produce a form of morphine, used to counteract dysentery and cholera. Old razor-blades were purloined for primitive surgery and bamboo canes were used to splint broken limbs.'

From January 1944 Colonel Mackenzie sent all badly sick cases from 3 Block to the hospital in 6 Block. These included one case of cholera, which he had failed to diagnose as such. The cholera patient was given a bed in the middle of the Beri-Beri patients. His neighbours contracted cholera. The Japs were informed. Isolation measures were taken. I cannot praise too

102

highly the dedication of Major Ramsay and his orderlies in dealing with the epidemic. This ran its course in 14 days. We were very lucky to lose only about ten men, whose corpses were burnt inside the jail walls. If cholera had obtained a real grip, it would have been 'curtains' for all of us. I remember that I knew there was cholera in 6 Block when I took out a work-party one morning. To avoid unnecessarily depressing everyone I did not divulge what I knew. I also remember on Colonel Mackenzie's initiative all of us in 3 Block 'swatting' flies for a couple of hours - a useless activity which was not repeated.

Despite the fact that from January 1944 all hospital cases were sent to 6 Block this did not mean that Colonel Mackenzie had little to do - far from it.

I remember observing from my bed opposite across the barrack room, when he extracted a tooth from Geordie Fullarton (a lieutenant in the Burma Frontier Force captured with his CO, Major Loring, and previously an executive with the Irrawaddy Flotilla Company). Fullarton had a most painful abscess, but they both had difficulty in deciding which tooth was infected. Hoping for the best, the Colonel selected one. Three heavy weights held poor Fullarton down. The Colonel tugged with huge forceps, lent by the Japs, and out came the tooth. The three heavyweights relaxed their grip and Geordie rose from his bed with a great shout of pain. There were no anaesthetics. Fortunately the correct tooth was extracted.

The Japanese allowed us to bury our dead in Rangoon Cemetery. The bodies were sown up in rice sacks, although later rough coffins were provided. The occupants of the compound would give a final salute to their dead comrade as his body was marched with an officer in the lead out of the compound.

2.   My own health record

WEEP AND YOU WEEP ALONE
LAUGH AND THE WORLD LAUGHS WITH YOU

These words in large capitals on a board dominated the room. I remember thinking how inappropriate they were. The words 'O ye who are damned enter here'[12] would have been more apposite.

It was early in 1944 and I was in the prison camp hospital. This was an old bug-ridden building situated in a compound of 6 Block. There was a sort of greenhouse staging all round on which lay the sick and the dying. I was lying on my front. I could not lie on my back. My backside was a mass of suppurating sores which itched terribly. Colonel Mackenzie had diagnosed my condition as 'scabies'. We had no medicine which was any use at all and the sores were spreading. He had decided to send me to the prison hospital.

Soon after my arrival my friend Captain Tiny Henstock, who as I have related was at that time Second-in-Command of 6 Block came down to greet me. Before he left, he bent down so that no one else could hear, and said to me quietly "I will work on Nigel (Loring) and Raymond (Ramsay) and get you out of here." Raymond Ramsay experimented with a solution of copper sulphate - Blue Stones - on my scabies condition. It was extremely painful, which did not worry me in the least. It was so much better than that dreadful itching and it was effective. I quickly started to improve. Tiny Henstock was as good as his word and after a few days I was moved up to the officers' barrack room. Raymond Ramsay continued my treatment there. However, before I was moved upstairs, I was able to observe the routine of the medical orderlies. At least once a day two of the orderlies would study the very sick. They were then moved around so that the one they expected to die first was at the end. From this position it was easier to sew the dead body in a sack for his funeral.

I stayed in 6 Block for a further two or three weeks. Always gregarious, I thoroughly enjoyed my stay, meeting so many new faces. One or two were exceptionally amusing, masters of our macabre humour.

I have recounted this episode at the beginning of this section as my arrival in that depressing hospital was one of the low points of my time in captivity. But to deal with my illnesses in chronological order, the first two were bouts of dengue fever in Moulmein Jail and in 'solitary.' I was able to throw both of them off after four or five days. But as I have recounted, the timing of the attack in 'solitary' during the broadcasting episode was fiendishly unlucky for me. Nevertheless the reader of the whole of my Memories will perhaps notice that on a number of occasions 'Lady Luck' was on my side.

Soon after Colonel Mackenzie took over as doctor in charge of 3 Block, I passed the dreaded blood and mucus in my stool. I reported sick. He diagnosed dysentery and put me in the room we used as a hospital. He gave me some revolting, useless concoction to drink and told me I must not eat anything. "Nothing more I can do for you." He said with satisfaction. Perhaps I was over-sensitive but the implication was that if I did not do as he said I would die - a state of affairs that I felt he viewed with some equanimity. Anyway it made me more determined than ever to throw off the dysentery, which I did.

I have already mentioned that in early 1945, after swimming in the polluted Rangoon River, I developed jaundice. I went yellow all over and lost my appetite. I do not remember taking any medicine. I certainly did not want to be sent over to the hospital in 6 Block. I did not feel that I had completely thrown off the after-effects of this illness when we marched out of Rangoon on 25th April. From time to time we were weighed by the Japs. I was the only officer not to lose weight. I had boxed at the Cadet College at Bangalore in the under nine stone weight. I was just over nine stone each time I was weighed. But I proved pretty quickly after our release that I would have put on weight over those years had I not been a prisoner.

H.   Our attitude to Japanese discipline

As I wrote at the beginning of this chapter, after our release from solitary and the departure of Captain Koshima, the behaviour of the guards changed for the better. In this section I will try to illustrate and explain our attitude to their disciplinary measures. I will start by describing a number of remembered episodes.

Hitting Colonel Power

I was hitting Colonel Power. I was not dreaming. I was actually striking him quite hard across his face with open hands. On either side of me other officers were doing the same to their comrades. We were in the garden behind No.3 Block, lined up in two ranks facing each other. The guard poised to intervene, was working himself up into a rage, shouting at us to hit harder. We had committed some offence - real or imaginary.

Afterwards, upstairs in our Block, I called out across the room.

"Of course I would have 'bashed' hell out of you Colonel - but I knew that it was your turn next to have a crack at me."

I am pleased to relate that the Colonel joined in the general amusement at my comments as I was sure he would.

Mota San and the old man from the Andaman Islands

I was leaving the latrines at the bottom of the compound when I heard that a Jap guard named Mota was beating up an old

106

man, an Anglo Indian civilian from the Andaman Islands, whose name I forget. He never seemed quite right in his head to me.

It was generally accepted that no one interrupted a guard beating up a prisoner. Early on, rare attempts to do so had resulted in a severe beating for both. But I felt that I could handle this particular guard and that if nothing was done the old man would only make matters worse by his confusion.

I walked up the compound 'with purposeful tread.' Some of the men looked up and watched. I went round the corner of the building, stopped in front of the guard and saluted, Mota was fuming with rage and shouting at the prisoner to 'keri.' The old man did not understand. His spectacles were on the ground. He seemed half-stunned by the slap across his face. Mota acknowledged my salute and waved me on. I changed my mind and did not speak the words which I had rehearsed. I climbed up the outside steps. When I was half way up, Mota stopped hitting the old man.

I justified my conduct to myself afterwards. By returning to the officers' room that way, which I had no need to do, and interrupting the guard to acknowledge my 'keri,' I did in fact achieve my objective. Although a number were aware that it was taking place, no one else felt any obligation to interfere with the beating up of this old man who in any event was a civilian and not one of our men. This as I have mentioned was settled policy. All this is true.

If I behaved so admirably, why is it then that I felt embarrassed when I read how Colonel Laurens Van der Post, in an infinitely worse situation, told the Japanese guard, 'Hit me instead'? Why is it that to my dying day I shall remember the words which I did not speak? I had intended to speak these in 'pidgin' Japanese with suitable explanatory gestures.

'Mota San. Nanaju ichi. Atama Warui.'

'He is 71 years old (this does not seem to me as old now

107

as it did then!) and his mind is bad.'

The truth is that at the last minute 'I passed by on the other side.'

[I stand by what I have written. Although I probably helped the old man, this was an occasion when I did not behave as creditably as I would have wished].

A fine start to a day

One early morning I was standing rigidly to attention in the front of the compound of No.3 Block, facing the Water Tower. The sentry was standing in front of the tower, glaring at me through the iron railings. His 'beat' was to patrol round the water tower. As he had rounded this into full view of our compound I had failed to notice him and did not 'keri' in time. It was uncharacteristic of 'an old lag' like me to get caught out in this way. But I was still half asleep.

I saw my friend Captain Tiny Henstock, walking down the outside steps of No.6 Block. When he saw who it was standing to attention, he exploded with laughter and gave me 'the thumbs up' sign. The sentry of course had his back to No.6 Block as he stood motionless in front of me. I had to remain still with my face as inscrutable as a Japanese.

At that moment I felt a sharp pain in my left ankle. I had been struck by a pebble rolled along the ground below the low brick parapet underneath the iron railings. Out of the corner of my eye, I could see two of my friends 'cackling away' out of sight of the sentry as they repeated their attacks.

I neither laughed nor moved; but I had some pretty indignant comments to make afterwards. For his part Tiny Henstock, when I next had the chance to talk to him, was equally unrepentant. He said that it had made his day, seeing me start mine in that fashion.
The soap episode

108

In early March 1945 some of the men discovered that one of the cells in the Punishment Block was being used as a store of soap for the Jap staff. They were working nearby and in their customary manner had 'smelt' something worth 'fiddling.' With commendable restraint, instead of taking a number of cakes at once, the loss of which would have been noticed, they contented themselves with two or three cakes a time. They also picked and replaced the lock each time.

Everything proceeded smoothly for a month or so, during which time perhaps 6 to 8 dozen cakes had been removed. Then disaster struck. The store attracted the attention of some of the Japanese troops, who raided it themselves, taking about a gross of cakes in one fell swoop and leaving a broken lock behind them. The loss was noticed at once by their Quartermaster and an enquiry held. To evade responsibility the Japanese soldiers blamed the British prisoners.

This led to a series of inspections, during which we were stood to attention outside in the compound for several hours at a time. The Japanese Quartermaster was determined to prove that it was the prisoners who had stolen all the soap. A few cakes were found and the owners were beaten up. It would have been worse had it not been for the courage of two of the men who confessed to having been responsible for taking the soap. They were badly beaten up.

The Japs seemed to accept what the two men had told them. The interpreter addressed us on behalf of the Commandant and said that he was surprised to find the British stealing - 'a bit rich' as we knew that two Japanese soldiers had been beaten up for this offence. We thought it was all over. With unbelievable stupidity, I recovered my piece of soap which I had buried in the garden. To my horror shortly afterwards we were turned out to stand to attention in the compound, while the Japs searched the

Barrack Rooms once again. It was very late in the afternoon. The next half hour was one of the most unpleasant in my life. I had hidden the soap in a seam in my old army greatcoat, when we were called out. It seemed inconceivable that they would fail to find it. I remember saying out loud: "Oh please God, let it get dark soon." When my comrades had recovered from their incredulity that I had been so stupid as not to destroy my piece of soap like everyone else, they were singularly unhelpful. A message for me was passed up from a friend at the other end of our two ranks. It was given to me amidst general laughter.

"Tell him it's getting lighter."

In fact this badinage, difficult although it may be for an outsider to understand, was helpful to me. It took my mind off my predicament. There is no doubt that as an officer in possession of stolen property after it was thought that the episode was over, I would have been severely beaten up. But my luck held. As soon as the Japs left the compound, I took a knife and the offending piece of soap into the latrines - and shredded it. [I chose the latrines as the garden was out of bounds after darkness].

I reflected afterwards that it was one thing standing up to beatings when we were in 'solitary' resisting Japanese demands and quite another to be half murdered as a receiver of stolen goods. The first would earn respect but not the second. The point is that we did not consider taking anything from the Japanese to be stealing. On the contrary, it gave us a sense of achievement and satisfaction. In this connection I was amused to be reminded of this episode when reading my friend Philip Stibbe's *Return via Rangoon*. He was also in possession for a time of 'some of the beastly stuff' as he called it. He describes how he got rid of it in colourful terms:

'I hid mine in various places about the compound but it seemed to shriek aloud wherever I put it; finally, I shredded it up and scattered it in the garden and when it was gone, I felt as if I had destroyed the last clue to a murder!'

110

I feel consoled to know that a distinguished school master was once a receiver of stolen goods like me![13]

The races

One morning shortly before we were marched out of Rangoon Jail we were diverted by the sight of the No.6 Block officers' garden party running round the central water tower, carrying canteen buckets, momates (hoes) and pushing wheelbarrows. Far from being sympathetic, some of us who knew many of the No.6 Block party, found it great fun. As they came into view out of sight of the sentry they had to listen to my running commentary:

"They are rounding Tattenham Corner now."

The reader may be shocked at the unsympathetic attitude to the minor punishments and humiliations which I have described. Probably one or two of the older officers did feel that we were hard and unsympathetic. But that was not the case when anyone was severely beaten up - a rare occurrence in the Jail after September 1942.

[There was however one exception to the improving behaviour of the guards. Private Koigotsu, known to the prisoners as 'Limpy' because he walked with a limp, was given 15 years imprisonment at the War Crimes trials in May 1946. He was quite frank in his evidence. "Yes, I beat the prisoners with my fists and with a wooden club taken from the limb of a tree because they failed to obey orders." I remember on one occasion when the officers were working in the Jail I noticed the officer in front of me as he went through a gap in a wall suddenly halt and do a 'keri' to his right. I followed and saw 'Limpy' standing in the shadows with his rifle butt raised to strike. I felt very naked as I quickly made my 'keri.' He did in fact use it once as we filed past but broke no

111

bones. But 'Limpy' was an exception and it was known that he was despised by the other guards].

I never had any doubt that our attitude was the best way of coping with the Japanese military discipline to which we were subject. It would have been pointless to indulge in self-pity or get indignant about minor humiliations. There were very few who did so. Nevertheless different ways were adopted in handling individual guards - very important when in charge of a work party. The first rule was never to show any trace of fear. Secondly, never to look down on them with a superior British officer look. They despised the first and hated the second. I usually started with the friendly smiling approach. Major Loring, who was quite fearless and very tough, achieved a great deal when in command of No.6 Block. He often made the guards laugh with his cheek and was always prepared to accept the odd beating up in the cause of those under his command. But the best was Warrant Officer Richardson of the RAF. Philip Stibbe writes:

'He had picked up the Japanese language with uncanny skill and he did splendid work at the docks, wheedling, soothing and cajoling the Japs into a more reasonable frame of mind.'

The anecdote of Mota San and the old man from the Andaman Islands provides an example of how I tried to handle Jap guards. Unfortunately it is an example of which I am not proud.

It is fair to point out that the Japanese soldiers were subject to the same discipline as us as the following extract from Colonel Power's diary for 24th April 1945 illustrates:

'That looting is suspected by the Japs was shown when the Jail guard started to take the law into their own hands this morning. A couple of Indians, probably quite innocent, but carrying bundles were beckoned to from across the road by members of the guard as they were passing the Jail entrance: they were then set-upon and beaten.

The commandant apparently witnessed the incident from

his bungalow. He came across and played merry hell with the guards, beating up each man in turn. Steel helmets and other equipment went flying all over the place. A good example of the Jap method of awarding summary punishment: it is very effective, though primitive.'

1.   Leisure Activities

I have always believed that I was born with two talents of which I have made insufficient use - the ability to play both chess and bridge to an above average standard.

I would very much like to have used up some of our leisure time playing chess. My father played it a lot during his four years in the trenches in the First World War. He taught me as a boy. I was good enough to win the Rugby School chess shield at the age of 16, but kept it pretty quiet as it was not considered a worthwhile achievement by my games-playing contemporaries. There was one set in 3 Block. This was owned by a character called 'Joe the Russian.' He was a civilian who had been incarcerated by the Japanese in Burma, presumably because he was a white man. I expressed the view that they should have treated him as an ally. His family had to flee Russia at the time of the Bolshevik revolution in 1917. Therefore as communist Russia was now at war with Japan, as a White Russian emigre he should be on the Japanese side. Neither Joe nor the Japanese agreed with me. A message came up that Joe would like opponents from the officers. Bill Gover, who came from an exceptionally keen chess-playing family, and I took it in turns to play him. Each of us just, but only just, had the edge over him. He was not prepared, however, to lend his set for us to play each other, which is what we wanted. Unfortunately 'Joe the Russian' and his chess set left Rangoon Jail for Tavoy with the other civilians in April 1943.

I played a great deal of bridge during my captivity. In

Moulmein I had taught three others how to play. In Rangoon there were several experienced bridge players. I mentioned two of these in my description of the bridge game interrupted by the bombs on the 28th November 1943. Another was Mr Waterfall who unfortunately for the better bridge players left for Tavoy in April 1943. We bridge players were not popular when we played after lunch, as we frequently did. We were accused on occasions of disrupting the important siestas of others! However my ultimate accolade as a bridge player was awarded to me when we were in India waiting to be repatriated for leave. I was asked by a fellow officer to join him in 'working the boats.' This was the phrase used in my school days to describe 'card-sharps' who used to travel on the big ships to and fro across the Atlantic. In fact what was suggested to me seriously by another officer, who did not even like me, was that we should travel home together by ship. He said that he had played a lot of bridge in the Army. We would be 'streets above' the average Army officer, who would be flush with money saved up during his months of fighting in Burma. In fact 'rich pickings.' I went home by air.

Much of my leisure time was taken up by reading. I have already referred to the conflict between smokers and readers in 3 Block. As some may be interested I include in Appendix B, an extract from Bruce Toothill's diary in which he listed the books read by him. It is not, in fact, comprehensive. For instance there were more than six of Charles Dickens's novels saved from the smokers. In particular I remember reading *Martin Chuzzlewit* which I considered to be the best. There were other books I can remember reading with pleasure, but perhaps these were among those consigned by Toots to utter oblivion. To be serious, in 3 Block we had a number of books which I enjoyed first reading and then discussing with others, Toots included.

A number of concerts in revue style were organised. I never played any part in them myself, but thoroughly enjoyed them.

The standard was very high. The producer was John Wilde, an officer in the Lancashire Fusiliers. He was extremely talented, as were many others. Philip Stibbe and John Kerr would appear as Colonels Bygadsby and Burrough Pegg, complete with monocles and Oxford accents. Their turn would consist of dialogue, anecdotes and songs in the manner of the Western Brothers (a well known comedy turn before the War). They would comment on topical events in a thoroughly scandalous and unrepeatable manner. The refrains of the songs were on the usual lines;

"Try to ignore it, you chaps!"

"It's all such a terrible bore!"

"Always give a 'keri' to the Nips, fellows!"

In the middle of one concert Private Williams, a brilliant mimic of the Japs, dressed as a Jap sentry stormed into the room. He shouted at the brigadier and delivered a tremendous tirade in pseudo-Japanese. The brigadier was not the only one taken in as he bowed and listened deferentially - that is until Private Williams ended his peroration with a list of punishments, all of which the victim was to be deprived of - 'Mishi' (food) NO! 'Misu' (water) No! 'Benjo' (!) No!"

I suppose, however, that my main way of passing our leisure time was in conversation. I cultivated fellow prisoners of different races, backgrounds and opinions. It was always a joy too when someone new appeared in the barrack room.

It is sad to relate that the five officers from 7 Baluch did not stick together in Rangoon Jail. If we had been allowed contact with our men, as of course the British Service Officers were with their BOR's, the shared responsibility could well have been a unifying factor. But as it was there was nothing to stop a clash of personalities - a common enough occurrence in Rangoon Jail. Two of the three Captains simply could not stand one another. Always outspoken, for a time I had problems with one of them. But this passed over and by the end I got on pretty well with all of them. But we had little in common with each other. We tended to join separate groups of friends. The exception, so far as I was concerned, was Toots. One of his three wounds had been a shot through his mouth knocking out some of his teeth and breaking his jaw. I had the greatest respect for the way he coped with the painful problems of eating (no solid foods) and drinking, particularly in the early months. He was some thirteen years older than me and had been a Director of Spencers, a large trading firm in Southern India (with the Connemara Hotel in Madras among its assets). He was free with his advice, which I sometimes took but generally did not treat too seriously! I used to spend an evening from time to time in 'Toothill Corner,' as he called it. The adjoining bed was occupied by another North countryman, Jack Wright, who had been the Navigator of a Wellington Bomber shot down in 1943. He became a lifelong friend but certainly not an Acolyte of Toots. I enjoyed Jack's sardonic wit. He tried to contact me when Toots died in the Isle of Man, his home, in January 1999 at the age of 90. Unfortunately we were abroad. Otherwise I would have joined Jack and his wife at the funeral.

Despite the background of hardship, coupled with Japanese military discipline, we did find a lot to amuse us. I will finish this chapter with two examples of the many incidents which I personally found amusing.

"Look at his toes."

On one occasion Mr Waterfall, the governor of the Andaman Islands complained to the brigadier about the rudeness and lack of cooperation on the part of one of his fellow prisoners, a wireless operator. As we were under military discipline this small rather 'bolshie' man was brought up before the brigadier and the adjutant. They heard the complaint in the corridor just behind my bed. Suddenly I was nudged by the occupant of the next bed who whispered: "Look at his toes."

I looked through the railings and observed an unusual exhibition of dumb insolence. The little man stared at Mr Waterfall throughout with an absolutely expressionless face. But he showed his contempt for each accusation by lifting both his large toes to an unbelievable extent. He was more than double-jointed. Then he would tap his large toes up and down as Mr Waterfall developed his complaint. We were the only two to notice.

The breathless hush

In Chapter X I referred to the volume of poems by Sir Henry Newbolt, which was the only book I had in solitary. One day a Captain Brown of the KOYLI, a rough diamond of an officer, who certainly had not been educated at an English public school, got his hands on the book. He then proceeded to read out the poem commencing:

> There's a breathless hush in the Close tonight,
> Ten to make and a match to win
> A bumping pitch and a blinding light
> An hour to play and the last man in.

He declaimed the poem in stentorian tones rising in a crescendo as he commenced the second verse with its fateful lines:

> The sand of the desert is sodden red,
> red with the wreck of a square that broke;
> The Gatling's jammed and the Colonel's dead
> and the regiment blind with dust and smoke.'
> He then lapsed into falsetto:
> 'But the voice of a school boy wallies the wanks
> Play up, play up and play the game.'

The recital was greeted with general mirth except from Bill Cayley of 7 Baluch - an Old Cliftonian - who growled "You are insulting my old school."

[On 24th September 1998, at a memorial gathering in London for John Butler DSO, I recounted this episode attempting to imitate the tones adopted by Captain Brown in his recital. At the time of his death in New Zealand, John Butler, a close friend since my Cambridge days, had been in correspondence with me helping to track down the text of this poem, not unexpectedly little known these days. He referred to it as *The Breathless Hush.* I subsequently discovered that its true title is *Vitae Lampada*].

A Solitary Confinment Cell, Rangoon Jail.

A Barrack Room in Block Three, Rangoon Jail.

119

A GROUP OF SICK PRISONERS LEFT BEHIND IN THE JAIL AS UNFIT TO MARCH

A GROUP OF PRISONERS WITH A UNION JACK, MADE FROM JAPANESE BLANKETS, CELEBRATING THEIR RESCUE - SOMEWHERE BETWEEN WAW & THE SITTANG BRIDGE

PART III

LIBERATION

For the wind is in the palm trees,
an' the temple bells they say:
"Come you back, you British soldier;
come you back to Mandalay!"

Mandalay   Rudyard Kipling

CHAPTER XIII

THE MARCH

During the early months of 1945 it became increasingly clear to us that the Japanese were losing the war in Burma. There were many reasons why we were confident of this.

The air-raids and fighter sweeps were growing larger and more frequent. We took this to be a sign of impending action.

I had spent the last three years discounting optimistic rumours which had always been a fact of life in Rangoon Jail. But as the weeks went by there were too many to ignore. Places like Mandalay and Meiktila were mentioned to work parties. Moreover there was the solid evidence of work parties observing a continuous exodus of troops and Japanese civilians from Rangoon.

Even 'Greater Asia,' the propaganda sheet, issued to us could not conceal the facts. No longer were there claims of victory at Imphal and talk of an impending Japanese invasion of India.

The Burmans in the streets were now much more friendly and would murmur to passing work parties. "It won't be long now." But how long? We were aware that the monsoon was due in early May. It would be my fourth since I was taken prisoner. Surely if there was any truth in the heartening rumours, our forces must be intending to take Rangoon before the onset of the monsoon rains?

It was an exciting time, but also one filled with apprehension. What would happen when our forces finally arrived? There were some who believed that the Japanese would kill us all rather than allow us to go free. Possibly in the days of Captain Koshima that would have happened. But most of us felt that with the war in Germany nearly over and Japan facing defeat, it was unlikely that the Japanese government would order a cold-blooded massacre. Nevertheless we could well find ourselves in the middle of a battle.

The atmosphere became more and more tense as the days in late April passed by. There were reports of rioting and looting in the town. We could hear shots being fired at night all over Rangoon.

Then on the 25th April, around midday, the Japanese informed us that all the British and American prisoners were to leave on foot by road for an unknown destination in four hours time. Only the very sick would be left behind. We would carry our own kit.

The Japs opened their store and issued us with all their surplus clothing. I selected a Japanese army shirt to replace my bedraggled, tattered army bush-shirt; but I decided against accepting a pair of Japanese canvas boots with rubber soles, preferring to remain barefoot. (Here I was wise as most of those who did developed blisters after a few miles and threw the rubber boots away).

Earlier that day the cooks had been given a number of pigs, more than it was possible to cook in the time.

The medical officers sorted out the sick, who were to remain in the Jail, from the rest of us, who were to march. I had not recovered fully from my attack of jaundice, but otherwise was reasonably fit by Rangoon POW standards. We were joined by a number of British and American airmen from No.8 Block. I have described earlier the way they had been treated by the Japs (see Chapter XII). They were pale and emaciated and in no condition to face the ordeal of the march. In fact the total distance which we were to cover in four marches (mostly at night) during the next four and a half days was about 65 miles.

I set out in the following two paragraphs an account of the organisation of the march as recounted by Colonel Power.

'The administrative arrangements consisted of cooked rice,

some beans and pork carried in the hand-carts for the evening meal, while the gaol lorry went ahead with uncooked rations and large empty barrels for boiling water.

We were in four groups; the working party of 200, under me; fit men of No. 6 Block under Nigel Loring; the remainder of the officers under Brigadier Hobson; and, in the rear, the Air force personnel, under the command of Captain Hunt, of the USAAF. The Jap escort comprised an advance guard of one NCO (with bicycle) and three men; a senior NCO with about three men to each group of 50 prisoners and, I presume, some sort of rearguard. The AM. went ahead with the lorry; the commandant with his staff marched at the rear. In addition, twelve men and an NCO marched ahead to arrange bivouac areas.'

There were some 400 of us in total. I was in Brigadier Hobson's group.

We moved off in the late afternoon. Some men were detailed to push the hand-carts loaded with Japanese kit and buckets and wooden tubs for our food and drink. The rest of us marched carrying our belongings - modest in my case, although I did carry a blanket.

We marched north up the Prome road. I remember that some of the tarred surface was softened from a day of unbroken sunshine. Although the soles of my feet had hardened over the last three years, I found it very uncomfortable for a time.

We marched at a slow pace with hourly halts of ten to fifteen minutes. After eight miles we halted for one hour - for a meal of rice, beans and pork fat. At about 1.00am some fourteen and a half miles from the jail we reached our destination. This was a mango copse a hundred yards from the road. I wrapped myself in my blanket and quickly fell fast asleep.

At 8.00am on 26th April we fell in for roll call. As so often with the Japs, this took a long time with several recounts. We then breakfasted on the remains of the evening rice and pork.

Colonel Power writes:

'Changing of the guard followed. It was carried out with parade ground ceremonial and seemed to take a ridiculously long time. There was a great deal of bowing, interspersed with animal-like grunts, probably expressions of devotion to the Emperor, first by the respective Guard Commander and then by all members of the Guard collectively.

Then followed the changing of the sentries, accompanied again by much grunting and bowing, and included the air sentry, posted some distance from the Guard and bivouac area. This man was draped in an individual camouflage net; it had a few leaves stuck into it here and there, but as it did nothing to break up the outline of the man or conceal his shadow, it must have been of little value.

One amusing feature of the Guard's arrangements was the Guard Commander's chair, always prominent in the guard house of the central jail. The Guard Commander always sat in it, with a sentry on his left, and except in the case of his own officers or NCOs, acknowledging salutes in the sitting position.'

All this caused us considerable quiet amusement, as the antics of the Jap guards so often did. It was a welcome distraction from the uncertain prospects before us. We were also concerned about our safety from air attack. The cover from aerial view was on the sparse side. We were told by the Japs to lie still if our aircraft passed overhead. We knew that we were not far from Mingaladon Aerodrome, a priority target. We were told that we had to remain there as it was no longer safe to move by day along the road due to allied fighter patrols.

We rested under the trees until about 6.00pm when we had a meal of rice and excellent pre-war chutney; half the rice had to be kept for the midnight halt.

We moved off as soon as it was dark. During the night

and early morning of 26th/27th April we covered 27 miles. At the junction of the Prome and Pegu roads by the 21st milestone at Taukkyan, we branched right on to the Pegu road. This convinced most of us that our destination was south Burma via Pegu and the Sittang Bridge. We stopped for our midnight meal of rice and hot tea. Shortly before dawn we reached Hlegu. But instead of bivouacking as we had all hoped and expected, there was another hour's halt and more tea. We reached our bivouac area at about 0930 hours.

The march had been exhausting for all of us; but for some it had been a nightmare. One officer, who had been marching in the same column as I was, fell out without any of us realising it. Others had asked to be put on one of the carts. But he was never seen again.

The road surface was reasonably smooth, but there was quite a lot of broken glass lying about. This was difficult to pick out in the moonlight. Several of those walking barefoot suffered cuts. My right toe beneath the nail became septic at that time. What originally caused it I cannot remember. I lost the nail. I know that it was the right toe, because to this day the replacement nail grows rough and disfigured; but it did not adversely affect my ability to walk.

Many of the Jap guards clearly found the march a strain. They became increasingly irritable.

Our bivouac area for the day of 27th April was a small hutted compound bound by a thick bamboo fence. It was very confined. There were three huts. One was taken by the Japs, the smallest allotted as the cook house and Colonel Power with 200 men under his command squeezed into the third. The officers party of which I was one laid out under the trees. We were not 'happy campers.'

As soon as they could the cooks produced a meal of rice, chutney and boiled gram. I settled down to sleep but it was not easy. For instance I was woken twice by the shouts of air sentries and the noise of aircraft. The first was a large formation of gleaming Liberators flying far lower than I had seen them over Rangoon. Later there was a squadron of fighters. We were relieved to see both lots pass over and disappear towards Rangoon.

Although we were all depressed by the rigours of the previous night's march and the gloomy outlook for the immediate future, most of us did our best to maintain a cheerful demeanour. For instance I remember that when we had turned right onto the Pegu road the previous night and were speculating as to how far we were going to have to march, I announced to my comrades that I had decided to change the title of my memoirs.[14] They were no longer going to be called 'Brigadiers I have known.' I had decided that a more appropriate title would be 'From Cockfosters to Tokyo.' But this witticism, if it deserves such a description, was uttered early on in the night's march. In its later stages, there was no conversation. We just marched - mile after mile, hour after hour.

There was one further meagre meal; then at about 2200 hours on 27th April we resumed our march.

The march during that night was quite a bit shorter than the previous night's. We were considerably delayed by allied night-fighters patrolling the road. Air-raid warnings were frequent; we would throw ourselves either in the ditch or find some other cover. Only once did a plane open up on us. Clearly the pilot had seen something of interest, as the plane circled around for what seemed an eternity. In the bright moonlight we crouched motionless with heads down. On this occasion I had found cover a little way away from the road. Someone beside me identified the plane as a Beaufighter. There was no machine gun fire as I, for one, expected, but a loud explosion. It was either canon fire or a small bomb. It landed among a convoy of bullock carts we had just overtaken.

As we marched nearer to Pegu, we could see ahead a

glow in the sky. There were rumbles from all directions. Abandoned cars and lorries became more frequent. The moon had set; the road now ran between dark plantations. It became very difficult to identify the potholes and the broken glass.

We had an hour's halt at 0200 hours and hot tea. Then we marched on and on, more and more slowly, despite the urging of the Jap guards, until daybreak. By this time there were few who were not utterly exhausted and many who were in constant pain from their feet cracking up. We were still a few miles short of the bivouac area prepared for us on the outskirts of Pegu. To move along the road in daylight was now a non-starter. We were drawn up in an open field, with the hand carts parked nose to tail on the road. The commandant reconnoitred some low bamboo and jungle-covered hills behind some deserted houses the other side of the road. [This was the place which I revisited in 1976 - see Appendix E].

We moved quickly into our allotted areas. With some others, I scrambled some way up a sunken road in the trees above the houses. Unbelievably the hand-carts were left lined up on the road. Almost immediately our fighter planes came over. They flew low along the road from the North. Of course they saw the hand-carts and they then turned their attention to our wooded hill. Each time they cruised overhead we lay still. On occasions they would screech down on top of us or along the road, firing their guns. In fact no one was hit; but it was a long, nerve-wracking, terrible day, made infinitely worse by the fact that it was our own planes which were machine-gunning us.

We were given a little rice and some golden syrup, but that was all for the day. Cooking was forbidden and there was no water.

The Jap guards behaved increasingly strangely. We were spread over a considerable area; but there were only one or two Japs on sentry duty. This was quite different from previous halts

128

during the march. The rest had disappeared into a house a little way away. They seemed to be taking no interest in us. Although I was unaware of it at the time, it was reported that the hand-carts were being abandoned and that the Japs were throwing away kit. Under the unprotesting eyes of the sentry, Colonel Power and others helped themselves from the hand-carts.

In the late afternoon I was sought out by a friend, another Second Lieutenant from the early days, Bill Gover of the 2nd/5th Royal Gurkha Rifles. He had remained with the remnants of his company all of whom were non-swimmers, when the Sittang Bridge was blown up. He told me that the possibilities of escape were being widely discussed and that one or two had slipped away into the jungle. He suggested that we might do the same.

I was no longer the enthusiastic, perhaps at times rather reckless, young officer, who would have joined in any attempt to seize the boat on its way to Moulmein. After enduring over three years of captivity, I wanted to survive and to enjoy life again. So far as I was concerned (but not Bill Gover), there was one over-riding consideration. It would be dishonest of me to pretend otherwise and these memories are a truthful account of my experiences - 'warts and all.' I applied my mind to the one question: Which course of action would give us the better chance of survival? [It is however fair to say that, as I recount later, once I was free I decided that after home leave I would return to active service in the war against Japan and I did not change my mind before the war suddenly ended].

There was a case for escaping while the opportunity was there. We knew that our forces were advancing from the North. It was a reasonable assumption that they would be aiming for Rangoon and doing their utmost to reach it before the monsoon arrived. It was true that once we were over the Pegu Bridge and had turned North-East towards the Sittang Bridge, we would be nearer our advancing troops. But the opportunity to escape might not arise. Once we had crossed the Sittang Bridge and turned South, it would have gone for ever and we could expect to spend another two years or so in Japanese prison camps.

On the other hand, without food or water in our present physical condition (walking barefoot in the jungle), we would almost certainly be dependent on help from Burmese villagers to achieve success. I remembered my experiences on the run after the battle of Pa-an. We expected that the attitude of the Burmans would have changed; but could we be certain of this? We did not know how near our forces were. Might they not be held up by the monsoon before reaching the Pegu area?

There was a further relevant factor in my case. I felt that I had coped pretty well with the rigours of the march, bearing in mind that I was one of those who had been captured early on and consequently had been longer on a debilitating diet and also that I was still recovering from my attack of jaundice. Nevertheless, towards the end of the previous night's march, I had started to feel the strain. My customary cheerfulness deserted me, and I remember being irritable towards my walking companions. Moreover the day with the continuous air activity I have described had not exactly proved restful. However this was a neutral factor. We would be hiding more often than marching if we escaped.

I also remember thinking that if we did decide to escape we should ask one or two other mutual friends to join us.

But I decided to stay with the marching party. In assessing the relevant factors, it never even crossed my mind that I had once given my promise to the Japanese not to attempt to escape. I gave my views to Bill Gover who accepted my decision. In fact we would not have escaped without first reporting our intention to the Brigadier who was in charge of our column. Although I was unaware of it at the time, the senior officers had met to discuss the possibilities of a mass escape. They had decided that the time was not right. Colonel Power, in particular, thought it would be madness to attempt it before we crossed the bridge at Pegu and we were nearer our advancing forces. The Brigadier would have appealed to us to stay. We would have accepted that.

[About thirty men did slip off into the jungle that day, including two officers. The officers were asked to join a party of Australian non-commissioned airmen. The leader was Flight Sergeant Harvey Besley, an Australian Airforce pilot. He was an absolutely first-class man who had done magnificent work in charge under Major Ramsey of the prison hospital in 6 Block. He was awarded the Military Medal for leading the escape. An account of this is included in his book entitled *Pilot, Prisoner, Survivor - Six Years in Uniform* which is in the Imperial War Museum. They planned the escape early in the day and obtained the permission of Major Loring, who was in charge of their group. Getting away was easy; then after a day or so trekking through the jungle they succeeded in finding a village without any Japs. The villagers gave them food and before long made contact with our forces. The escape was not without its alarms and excursions].

Soon after dark on 28th April the Japs returned and we resumed the march. We left behind the hand-carts. This meant that the sick who had been able to ride on them for a time now had to be helped along by their comrades. This slowed us down even more. The Japs were to become increasingly impatient as the night wore on.

We passed through Pegu. The town was in ruins. We crossed the bridge over the river. We observed that it was being prepared for demolition. On the far outskirts of Pegu, we left the road and marched up a rough path which ran beside the railway line. We passed through Waw and then turned East following the line of the railway towards the Sittang Bridge.

[I have subsequently learned from the Baluch History that my old battalion after 10 days marching from the North down the Rangoon Road had halted earlier that day at Milestone 54 1/3, only 4 miles North of Pegu. In fact we must have been even nearer our forces as we marched up to and through Waw].

At the point where we left the road a Squadron-Leader with 8 Block party at the rear of the column fell out. It was reported that a Jap guard had butted him in the stomach with a rifle. He was last seen lying on the ground with the Jap medical orderly bending over him.

The going was very rough. At times the path petered out and we had to walk along the railway tracks. The moon shone brightly. This made it easier to pick out the many patches of thorny creeper and to navigate the uneven terrain. It also meant that we had to drop down and lie flat whenever planes flew overhead. Apart from my septic toe, which did not really inconvenience me, my hardened feet held up admirably: but many were suffering grievously. Colonel Mackenzie's feet had become semi-paralysed. He was unable to walk any further and was being carried along between two of the cooks. Perhaps I was not so selfish and unsympathetic, as some might infer from my writings, because I suddenly felt terribly sorry for 'the old man,' as we called him, in such a pitiable condition. I gave him my precious water bottle to have a drink. I had not intended however that he should pretty-well drain it! But he did not realise what he was doing. No water had been issued for 24 hours. The Japs would not allow us to stop at any of the few pools of water which we passed. Amazingly however one or two of the guards handed round their water-bottles.

Shortly before dawn, the Brigadier told the Commandant that there were many who could not march any further. "We must have a rest, food and water." Surprisingly the Commandant accepted this and sent one of his men forward to find a suitable place. Soon we crossed the railway and moved to a well-wooded hamlet adjoining the Naung Pattana Station. This proved to be our final bivouac.

CHAPTER XIV

RESCUED

It was now daylight in the early morning of 29th April 1945 - a fateful day in my life. As soon as the Japs allowed us to fall out, most of us moved quickly to find comfortable places under the trees in which to lie down and try to sleep. Suddenly everyone stopped what they were doing. I looked up and saw the Brigadier striding through the glade. He climbed a fallen log. Then in a loud, clear voice he spoke these words: "At last I can tell you something that you have been waiting for for years: we are all free men."

A great cheer went up and we all rushed around congratulating each other. It would be impossible to exaggerate the feeling of euphoria which we all shared. From steeling ourselves to face up to and to endure more strain, more hardships, we now suddenly and unexpectedly had this wonderful vision of freedom. We could look forward to civilised life once again and of eventually returning to our homes and families.

The Commandant had sent for the Brigadier as soon as we arrived at the village and informed him that he was going to release us. He advised us to stay where we were. Our troops would rescue us in a day or so. He gave the Brigadier a note in Japanese stating that we had been officially liberated. He told the Brigadier to show this to any Japanese troops we encountered. He then shook hands with the Brigadier and moved away with his party 'like bats out of hell' in Colonel Power's words.

The senior officers began to organise what needed to be done to make secure our new-found freedom. The immediate danger was from our aircraft and our top priority to make contact with them. We were ordered to keep under cover. Using all available white clothing, including Japanese underpants given to us before we left Rangoon, a ground strip message was laid out. It read '400 White POWs Ex Rangoon now free here: send help: drop radio.'

An American airman said that they had been trained to contact their aircraft in such circumstances. He lay down beside the strip and started to signal with a small piece of mirror.

Soon our encampment was full of villagers. They seemed very friendly and were full of promises of food and firearms, although in fact they produced little of either.

During the next hour or so several planes flew over at high altitude ignoring us. There was an outburst of firing a hundred yards or so away. The villagers said that this came from a small party of Japs who were trying to intimidate villagers to produce bullocks. A tremendous artillery barrage started to the north-east, some shells landing only about a mile or two away. During this time, we chatted excitedly amongst ourselves while watching the distant battle. We were confident that our signals would be seen before long and were prepared to wait a little longer. The cooks started to prepare a meal from a small amount of rice and a few sweet potatoes provided by the villagers pooled with our remaining onions and gram. Our last meal had been some 48 hours earlier, and we had eaten nothing of substance for much longer.

Suddenly four fighter planes flew over much lower than hitherto. They circled even lower. Some men stood by the ground strip and waved a piece of cloth. We watched hopefully as they circled above us. Surely they must have seen and read our message? There was a burst of machine gun and canon fire. Forgetting all our ailments we ran away from the houses and the centre of the bivouac area. I found some sort of cavity in the ground and piled in with several others. Bullets sprayed the trees above us and the ground beside us. Eventually after several runs the planes flew off.

Although there were four hundred of us in a fairly small target area, amazingly there was only one casualty. The Brigadier, who had established his HQ in one of the empty houses, was killed outright. It was a cruel piece of fortune.

Colonel Power writes:

'A few minutes later the whole area sprang to life. Half naked men, singly or in small parties, streamed across the paddy fields; one party ran to a village, five or six miles away before they stopped.'

In fact few of us wanted to remain in the village. We felt that there must be a risk of further air attack. [I was told later that a force of light bombers (Mitchell B25s) were turned back en route for this target. Apparently one of the fighter pilots had noticed our ground strip and reported that there was something unusual about the place].

With one or two others I went out into the middle of the paddy field. It was unbearably hot with no protection from the sun. After a time, there having been no further air attacks on the bivouac area, some of us returned. We spent the day nearby. Major Loring was in command of us. He rearranged the ground strip message into a large SOS. We were now spread out over a large area. Colonel Power, who was in overall command following the death of the Brigadier, and the rest of the prisoners who were in fact the majority gradually assembled at a nearby village where food and accommodation had been offered.

After the strafing, the need to make contact with our troops became the top priority. Major Lutz of the USAF volunteered to find his way across country to where our troops were thought to be. We could see supply dropping six or seven miles away. He set off early in the day on his own initiative, disguised as a Burman with a Chinese youth as guide. In the afternoon he succeeded in making contact. Just as we were settling down for the night he reappeared. He told us that a company of Indian Infantry and transport for about 200 were waiting for us nearby. We all owed him a great debt of gratitude and I hope that he was suitably

135

rewarded by the British for his courage and initiative.

I was among the first to be escorted across country to the rendez-vous. An Indian soldier came out of the darkness and shook my hand. We then boarded trucks and half an hour later we were being warmly greeted by the officers and men of a battalion of the West Yorkshire Regiment who were in 99 Brigade part of the 17th Indian Division. After a wonderful meal, almost certainly provided at considerable sacrifice on the part of our hosts, who were on short rations supplied by air, I wrapped myself in a blanket and lay down on the ground. Before I fell into a deep sleep, I gave myself time to reflect on the almost unbelievable fact that I was now a free man and a very lucky and happy one.

Rangoon
29th April, 1945.

To the whole captured persons of Rangoon jail.

According to the Nippon military order, we hereby give you liberty and admit to leave this place at your own will.

Regarding food and other materials kept in this compound, we give you permission to consume them, as far as your necessity is concerned.

We hope that we shall have an opportunity to meet you again at battlefield of somewhere.

We shall continue our war effort eternally in order to get the emancipation of all Asiatic Races.

Harwo Oto
the chief officer of Rangoon Branch Jail.

MESSAGE LEFT BY THE JAPANESE WHEN THEY ABANDONED RANGOON JAIL.

AERIAL PHOTOGRAPH OF RANGOON JAIL AFTER THE JAPANESE HAD LEFT.
THE MAIN ENTRANCE. NO. 1 BLOCK [WITH MESSAGE ON ROOF].
NO. 2 BLOCK AND NO. 3 BLOCK [AT TOP.

137

CHAPTER XV

THE FIRST FEW WEEKS OF FREEDOM

I slept well into the morning of 30th April. I was only briefly awakened by gunfire and shouted commands in the early hours. Apparently some Japs had infiltrated the perimeter. They were all eliminated without any casualties on our side. Times had changed from February 1942. In fact we were all astounded by the difference in the 17th Indian Division from those far-off days. It was not only the strength of its weaponry and the excellence of its organisation but even more the spirit and sheer confidence of its supremely fit officers and men which so impressed us.

Those prisoners who were not rescued with me on the previous evening spent an anxious day on 30th April. Many were in outlying villages. They had to hide from parties of retreating Japanese troops. Contact was eventually made; and in the evening all had been brought in to join us.

The next few days passed quickly for me. We were debriefed in turn, issued with clothes and medically examined. My septic toe was treated and quickly healed. Hugh Mercer, Bill Cayley and I were visited by George Holden. I had last seen him, strolling around with his tommy gun at the ready, organising a strong point near Battalion Headquarters shortly before the end of the Battle of Pa-an. I noticed with an unexpected pang of jealousy that he was now a Major. Clearly the years of captivity had not completely destroyed the competitive streak in my nature. He gave us a full account of the activities of the Battalion since the battle of Pa-an - more and more successful as time went by. We in turn told him of our experiences.

It was remarkable that 3¼ years after my capture my own

battalion should be in action so near to us. I have already mentioned that they were only four miles away when, having passed through Pegu, we left the road and followed the railway to Waw. On 30 April, my first day of freedom, 7 Baluch, now with 68th Brigade, attacked and secured the whole of the North East of Pegu comprising the residential area. Major John Randle was awarded the Military Cross. That night the Japanese pulled out of Pegu. The Battle of Pegu was the last heavy fighting by the battalion. They had hoped with the 17th Indian Division to be the first to enter Rangoon but that was denied them. In the afternoon of 1st May a torrential storm burst over the whole area. The monsoon had arrived early. Rangoon was taken from the sea on 2nd May. The Baluch history relates:

"But if they were disappointed in this (especially the very few who had been with the battalion throughout its campaigns in Burma) they had the great joy of hearing of the release of several of the officers captured at Pa-an. These were Captains WB Cayley, CH Mercer and Lieutenant[15] CRL Coubrough who along with some 400 others had been abandoned by their guards while being marched towards the Sittang."[16]

When the advance was halted by the rains, John Randle asked for permission to visit us; but this was refused. Major George Holden was DAA&QMG (in my day Staff Captain) with 99 Brigade which had rescued us. As I have described he came to welcome the three of us.

A further history of the 10th Baluch Regiment is at the present time being written by a Major-General Rafiudin Ahmed in Pakistan. He has been in correspondence with John Randle and other Baluch officers.

I have recently discovered a number of letters which I wrote over the next few weeks to my parents. The first was written in pencil as early as 30th April and began:

'At last I'm back in circulation again and about time too!

139

The Japs in their usual pleasant manner decided to move all 'fit' prisoners from Rangoon on the 25th, at the very last minute and by marching. I will tell you about it later, but even for me who was comparatively fit, it was pretty tough.'

These letters (together with a diary kept by Bill Gover) have enabled me to record reasonably accurately my peregrinations throughout India in the next few weeks. My letters also record my actual thoughts at the time. It is perhaps not surprising that with the excitement of freedom after the dark years, my memory of the events of those weeks (except for certain specific episodes) is less clear than it is for the events of the previous three years. The time seemed to pass in a dream.

With a number of others I flew out from a dusty airstrip in a Dakota on the 3rd or 4th May to Comilla, a military staging post in Bengal. We were put in an hospital there, the first of three - in my view all unnecessary in my case. I remember attending a dinner to celebrate the end of the war in Germany as a guest in the officers' mess - quite an occasion. We went from there to Chittagong and then by sea to Madras. I quote below from a letter which I wrote on 18th May to my parents from the hospital there.

'We have come here by ship: quite a pleasant voyage, excellent food. We met no submarines or anything exciting. ... There are a few minor flies in the ointment of being free - one has to wear clothes and shoes. A piece of cloth and bare foot was far cooler and pleasanter! Also my first hospital bed was so soft that I seriously considered wrapping myself in a blanket and lying on the floor. I am certain I would have slept better.'

The hospital which we reached in the early evening of 16th May was at a place called Avadi outside Madras. Many of us were fed up with being treated as invalids. The next morning several of us decided to visit Madras for lunch. With Captain Henstock in the lead and ignoring the protests of the hospital staff, we stormed out of the hospital. We walked to the nearby station. There we boarded the guard's van of a local train bound for the centre of Madras. We then went by taxi to the Connemara Hotel. I wrote in my letter: 'India is very different from what it was in '41. We were only allowed three courses for lunch. That must shake some of the fat civilians here! [I remembered the occasion when as a newly commissioned Second Lieutenant a week or so after my 20th birthday en route to join 7 Baluch in Madras in September '41 I consumed a seven course meal at a station restaurant while the stationmaster held up the crowded train]. ... The drink situation is serious too! I hope Dad's got a good stock of beer at home!' Although there may have been a shortage of beer at the Connemara Hotel, I do remember that I acquired a taste that day for gin and ginger beer as a thirst-quenching midday drink. [There were no repercussions as a result of our going AWOL (absent without leave). Not that any of us gave the possibility a thought. In all honesty I for one simply did not give 'a damn.' But in fact shortly after our abrupt departure Major Ramsay, using his experience of negotiating with the Japanese, succeeded in persuading the bureaucratic medical officer in charge of the hospital to countermand his orders and allow the officers to go into Madras].

The next hospital was Secunderabad where I remained for over a week. From my letters it appears that we were all becoming increasingly exasperated by the red tape and lack of decision as to our future (i.e. when could we go home on leave and for how long)! But at the end of the month I was passed fit and given permission to visit the 10th Baluch regimental centre at Karachi for 48 hours before flying home on leave. In fact despite the frustrations, I had a very pleasant time in Secunderabad, treating the hospital as a hotel. I swam a lot at the officers' club with my friends and one Sunday spent the whole day yacht racing (in 16x6' Moths). I write below an account of a hockey match which took place at the hospital.

'As we walked on to the pitch carrying unaccustomed hockey sticks, a voice cried out:

"Come on lads. Let's fix the ......s. It's our last chance."

The officers were playing the other ranks at hockey on a pitch at Secunderabad Hospital against medical advice. The teams were drawn from those who had marched out from Rangoon Jail some three or four weeks earlier. Most of them I recognised as being from the early 1942 intake of prisoners. The voice was that of a tall lance-corporal from a Yorkshire regiment, who it was rumoured was an ex-light-weight boxing champion of the army. He waved his hockey stick around his head to emphasise his words.

In the event the match, although lacking in skill and resulting in an easy victory for the officers, was played in an excellent spirit. There was a mutual respect which had nothing to do with rank. After over three years of captivity culminating in the march out of Rangoon, we had found the energy to play a hockey match. We were the survivors.'

My reasons for visiting the 10th Baluch regimental centre in Karachi were as follows:

1.   To find out about my prospects on my return from leave and for the future in the unlikely event of my wanting to stay in the army.

2.   To sort out my pay.

3.   To ascertain the whereabouts of the large ant-proof tin trunk containing my 'civvy kit' which had been sent there. [In fact on arrival I found that it had been sent to Jhansi and from there in January 1945 shipped to Liverpool].

En route to Karachi my plane, an inevitable Dakota touched down at Nagpur. I wrote:

'A charming place - it is called the city of snakes: it is a strong Congress centre of unrest: there was a cholera epidemic raging and last but not least the temperature was 115 degrees in the shade. Also you got no beastly green grass around. Everywhere

TEL AVIV, 21ST JUNE 1945
ROBIN STUART (1ST/3 GURKHAS), MAJ. RAYMOND RAMSAY (R.A.M.C.),
C.R.L.C., JOHN WILDE (LANCASHIRE FUSILIERS).

is nice and brown.'

There I met a friend of my age with whom I used to play golf as a junior at Hadley Wood before the war. He told me that nine holes of the golf course had been dug up early on in the war. 'This is terrible news' I wrote. (In fact at that time Hadley Wood GC had 27 holes as I knew well and it was not as serious as I indicated!)

At the 10th Baluch regimental centre I learnt of the reputation of the 7th Battalion. I wrote home:

'The 7th/10th has a terrific name now. I want to get back to it when I finish my leave.'

In fact the two atom bombs were dropped and the Japanese surrendered while I was still on leave. It is however highly unlikely that I would have succeeded in rejoining 7 Baluch. My letters do however reveal my determination to return to active service in the war against Japan, but after a lengthy leave in England which was my top priority and which I clearly needed to recharge my batteries.

My letters do not reveal any bitterness about the way the Japanese treated us - that is after the departure (in September 1942) of Captain Koshima - 'an absolutely unmitigated swine as Commandant over us who encouraged the guards to hit prisoners.'

Despite the red tape and the indecisiveness of the authorities, due primarily to the fact that we were unexpected, none of us will forget the kindness and hospitality shown to us during those few weeks in India by almost everyone we met.

In mid-June I flew back to England in yet another Dakota - overcrowded and cramped. After a stopover at Tel Aviv we landed in the afternoon at an aerodrome in Somerset. It was a sunny, windy day as I descended the steps onto English soil. I immediately started to sneeze. I sneezed and I sneezed and I sneezed. The hayfever which had been absent since June 1940 had decided to welcome me back to England.

Late that night from the hotel in London to which we had all been sent, I was able for the first time since December 1940 to talk with my parents on the telephone.

The next day, 24th June 1945, I arrived home (Ardoch, Cockfosters, near Barnet in Hertfordshire) in time to take part unexpectedly in a tennis party arranged for my brother Ian who was on leave from Germany.

TENNIS PARTY AT HOME, 24ᵀᴴ JUNE 1945, IN PHOTOGRAPH TAKEN BY MY MOTHER, C.R.L.C., MY SISTER JOAN (AGED 11), MY FATHER (STANDING ON THE LEFT OF THE HAMMOCK) AND MY BROTHER, IAN (SITTING IN THE HAMMOCK).

No longer a Second Lieutenant!
C.R.L.C. in August 1945

146

CHAPTER XVI

FINAL REFLECTIONS AND SUBSEQUENT EVENTS

I have sometimes been asked what was my attitude to the Japanese during my imprisonment. This changed as time went by. I had no complaints about my treatment at the time of my capture or during the days which followed. Resentment grew as we were half-starved in Moulmein Jail and then shipped to Rangoon in horrible conditions. But it was while I was in solitary confinement under the regime of Captain Koshima from 26th June to 8th September 1942 that my feelings towards the Japanese became those of hatred and even more of defiance, but naturally defiance concealed from the Japanese except when they started to pressurise us to agree to broadcast.

However, after we came out of 'solitary' and life in 3 Block settled down into a routine as I have described, my attitude changed again. I no longer hated the Japanese and it was pointless to maintain a defiant attitude for years. Instead the Japanese guards in general became the objects of our ridicule and indeed of our contempt. We referred to them disdainfully as 'Japs' or more often 'Nips,' as they strutted pompously around, the representatives of the great Nippon, and demanded instant obedience to their every whim. There were of course exceptions; but I made it part of my settled policy not to try to become too friendly with any individual Japanese guard.

But if we looked on the Japanese with scorn, how much more so did they despise us? By allowing ourselves to be taken prisoner, in the eyes of the Japanese soldier we had forfeited all respect. They made no distinction between those few who perhaps had given up the struggle too easily and, say, the British officers in the Gurkhas who had chosen to remain with their non-swimming troops in order to share their hardships and spurned the opportunity of swimming the Sittang River to safety, or the Chindit officer left behind in the jungle with a bullet in his chest, or the New Zealand fighter pilot whose plane crashed into the ground leaving him unconscious but alive. We were all dishonoured men.

In the years after the war, apart from keeping up with friends, I did not give a great deal of thought to the war or to my time as a prisoner. I harboured no bitterness against the Japanese. Like so many others I just got on with my life, although I was not unaware of the fact that the experiences of those years had had their effect on me. I did know, however, that these effects in the terms of human experience were by no means all harmful. The worse conditions were, the more we sustained each other with friendship and humour, even if such humour might seem macabre or even black to readers who never shared our experiences. I saw no point in encumbering myself with resentment over past treatment.

I have related how as I grew older I gradually became more and more interested in the events of those war years. I read quite a lot about the Japanese and slowly changed my views. We had observed how blows of all kinds were the commonest form of discipline in the Japanese army and were frequently passed down from sergeant to corporal to private soldier. To a Japanese soldier this was part of every day life. The Japanese chose to consider that, since all prisoners had to obey the guards, they ranked lower than the first year private who was the lowest form of life in the Japanese army. This was reinforced by the teaching he had received that those who surrendered rather than fighting to the death were dishonoured men. It can be understood how these guards reacted toward the prisoners when encouraged to do so by Captain Koshima and his right-hand man the sadistic 'Little Corporal.' But

148

most of these guards behaved quite differently when Captain Koshima had departed and the 'Little Corporal' had been killed. For instance I remember that 'Blackie,' who had quite severely beaten me up in 'solitary,' was still in the jail when I was sent to the hospital in 6 Block in early 1944. I had come across him several times. He was always perfectly correct and easy to deal with.

I must also make the point that few, if any, of the warring nations posted their best men to prisoner of war camps as guards.

I read about the courage and tenacity of purpose of the Japanese armed forces. I observed how Japan had recovered from the ravages of total defeat. I no longer looked upon them with disrespect. Therefore when in late 1992 I was asked to join the Burma Campaign Fellowship Group (BCFG) whose aim was 'to encourage reconciliation between those who fought against each other in Burma in World War II,' I was happy to do so. It was 50 years since I had been taken prisoner and I felt that it was high-time to call it a day, to forgive and where possible to forget the past. I have not changed my views.

The BCFG and the comparable association of Japanese War Veterans, the A-BVAJ Association of Japan, arranged exchange visits between the two countries. These were funded largely by GB-Sasakawa Foundation of Japan.[17] I was invited to visit Japan as a member of two visiting parties, but declined both, the first on account of June's health after a serious operation and the second due to my own increasing arthritis. I did, however, attend two functions in London when the Japanese veterans came to London in September 1994.

My first contact was at the Forum Hotel. I quote from a short account I wrote at the time:

"Ho, ho, ho." laughed the elderly Japanese gentleman, pointing at my knees. "Ho, ho, ho, did we do that to you?" I was struggling to my feet to greet him as he advanced across the room. The Japanese were very jolly and friendly. One asked me where I had fought. I replied "At the Battle of Pa-an but two days later I was taken prisoner and spent the rest of the War in Moulmein and Rangoon Jails." Was I being over-sensitive or did the jollity vanish from his face? Did I detect a note of reserve in his voice? If this was the case - and I believe it was - what was the reason?

[It is perhaps relevant to mention that at that time members of the BCFG and of the A-BVAJ Association of Japan were for the most part former frontline fighting troops. There had been hatred between them, yes, but also mutual respect. I was the only ex-POW from the fighting in Burma. I have described the Japanese soldiers' contempt for us. It is true that there were a few other ex-POWs as members, most of whom suffered far worse conditions than I ever did. But they were taken prisoner at Singapore where they were ordered by General Percival to surrender. Even if at the time there was perhaps little difference in the attitude of the Japanese towards individual prisoners ordered to surrender at Singapore and those captured in Burma, I feel that the Japanese veterans in 1994, who had themselves surrendered by order of the Emperor, must have made a distinction].

I have little doubt about the reason. It was that the Japanese ex-officer had not changed his opinion that it was dishonourable to surrender rather than fight to the death. Why should he? British officers have their code of honour. Any officer who breaks that code (e.g. by running away from a battle) could not expect it to be forgotten. The Japanese had their own code of honour which put death before surrender. I no longer have any problems with the Japanese attitude on this subject. I understand it. Moreover I felt strongly that these honourable, friendly ex-officers would never have approved of the conduct of Captain Koshima or more particularly of the treatment of Allied aircrew in Burma in 1944 and 1945.

This brings me to the issue of an apology by the Japanese for the way they treated prisoners of war and internees. By

September 1994 there had been apologies, albeit rather unforthcoming and grudging. But since then apologies or expressions of sorrow have rained in from all directions - from the Emperor at a banquet given by the Queen, from the Japanese government following Prime Minister Blair's visit to Japan, from former Ambassador Kazuo Chiba who said on BBC TV's 'Newsnight' "I feel very sorry. I feel the actions by our people - the individuals involved - at that time were beastly. I am very sorry about it." And not least from Mrs Nobuko Kosuge at the War Memorial in the cemetery at Cambridge on Remembrance Day 1996 (see Appendix G). I feel strongly that we should accept them and stop going on quibbling over words.

On Saturday, 19 August 1995 a Service of Remembrance and Commitment was held outside Buckingham Palace to mark the 50th anniversary of the end of the Second World War. It culminated in the march down the Mall past The Queen. The Japanese were excluded from all the official VJ Day ceremonies, although the Heads of State of Germany and Italy were invited. There was no mention of reconciliation. To many Japanese, and in particular to some who had been promoting reconciliation between those who fought against each other in Burma, this was a matter of extreme sadness. While I understood and sympathised with their feelings, I did not look upon it in the same way. In my opinion the decision of the government to exclude the Japanese was inevitable, given the intense anger still prevailing in the British Legion, the Burma Star Association, the Far Eastern Prisoners of War Association and other associations about the treatment of prisoners of war and internees by the Japanese, all of which was reflected, often very unfairly, by the media. It was also a one-off event. There may have been damage to the reconciliation process but such damage was temporary and not irreparable. Moreover there was a Service of Thanksgiving at Westminster Abbey on Sunday, 20th August 1995 at which the Japanese were asked to participate together with members of the BCFG. The Dean of Westminster preached forgiveness and reconciliation. Since then, at the request of the BCFG, services of reconciliation have been held every year on the Sunday after the anniversary of VJ Day. In fact the reconciliation process has recently received considerable momentum by the successful state visit of the Emperor and Empress of Japan in May 1998. One can ignore, as the media should have ignored, the ill-mannered rudeness and discourtesy of a handful of 'veterans' seeking to insult publicly the head of state of a friendly country invited by us as our guest.

It is over 50 years since the end of the war against Japan. More and more of those of us still alive who fought in this war have stopped looking back in anger over the past and are holding out the hand of friendship to Japan.

The service outside Buckingham Palace and in particular the march down The Mall in front of cheering crowds thanking us for fighting for them was a wonderful experience which I shall never forget. It included looking straight into the face of The Queen, smiling broadly and obviously enjoying the occasion, as we saluted her with an 'eyes left.' For me it was a particular pleasure to march with former officers of the 10th Baluch Regiment, in which I served for such a short time but which meant so much to me.

This was the last of the events I have described to be attended by me personally. It is therefore fitting that it should provide the epilogue to my Memories which follows.

EPILOGUE

On Saturday, 19th August 1995 I marched down the Mall past Her Majesty The Queen. I marched with a borrowed bowler hat, a borrowed shooting stick and even borrowed medals (the correct ones!) but I marched with pride. I was proud to have been in action, however unsuccessfully, with 7 Baluch who became such a fine battalion in the British-Indian 14th Army. Under the command of General Slim this Army first held and then finally destroyed one of the most formidable fighting forces the world has ever seen.

The moving service outside Buckingham Palace which had preceded the march was a time to remember my friends and comrades who had been killed in the battle of Pa-an and those fellow prisoners of war who had either died in Rangoon Jail or afterwards at a young age as a result of the conditions there. It was a time also to remember my many friends whose cheerfulness and humour when times were bad had helped me to survive.

On Sunday, 20th August 1995, members of the Burma Campaign Fellowship Group were invited to a Service of Reconciliation at Westminster Abbey. June and I would certainly have attended if we had been at home. I saw no conflict between the two events. But we were on holiday with the family and I had to make a choice. Without in any way lessening my desire for friendship between Great Britain and Japan, I marched with my former comrades in arms.

153

RANGOON REUNION, EARLY 1960s: THE FOUR ORGANISERS AND TWO PRISON DOCTORS.
LEFT TO RIGHT:
BACK ROW CAPTAIN W. WILDING, C.R.L.C., CAPTAIN J. HARVEY.
FRONT ROW: COLONEL MACKENZIE R.A.M.C., COLONEL POWER, MAJOR RAYMOND RAMSAY R.A.M.C.

The old Coach House,
Wellisford.
Wellington,
Somerset
TA21 0SS

1st November 1998

Major General Rafiuddin Ahmad
21 Askari Villas
Chaklala Scheme III
Rawalpindi,
Pakistan

WORLD WAR TWO
HISTORY - 7ᵗʰ BN, BALUCH REGIMENT

Dear General

I am writing to correct some imprecision in the second paragraph of my letter to you of 23ᵗʰ October, which I would like to correct please.

It is true, in an historical sense, that Charles Cambrough was taken prisoner in the general context of the Battle of Paan/Kuseik, as opposed to the Sittang River Battle, Battle of Imphal or any of the other battalion fighting. However geographically, he was captured some distance from Kuseik, on the River Donthami two days later, after a determined and indeed valiant attempt to escape. It is an important distinction.

With many good wishes

Yours sincerely

John Randle

Hony Secretary Major M G Farrant, Kingswell House, Crawley, Winchester, Hants SO21 2PU
Telephone 01962 776386

A MESSAGE FROM BRIGADIER J.P. RANDLE O.B.E., M.C.

155

APPENDIX A

Document handed to officers in solitary confinement
on 13th August 1942

1. The Great Japan, since she was constructed about 3,000 years ago, has never been defeated by any other foreign country, so in this war no Japanese person thinks at all that their country will be defeated nor even has the slightest fear of it.

Hakko-wo Ie-to-nasu is a sentence, quoted from the Jimmu Tenno's edict, the first Emperor, that means 'You shall cover the world by one house,' that is our purpose in this war.

2. In the war 1914-1919 (sic) Japan observed faithfully the Japanese-British-Military-Treaty and fought hard for the allied countries.

In the conference at Versailles the reward, for the Japanese hard efforts, was too small. After the great war the British and American policies to Japan were extremely brutal. In the Washington Naval Conference they succeeded not only in compelling the Japanese Navy to adopt the ratio of the total tonnages of the Principal battleships 5:5:3 but also to settle the limited defence area, in the west half of the Pacific Ocean, they applied much limit on Japan and hardly any on their own side.

Thus the Japanese nation burnt with indignation and determined in their minds to conquer Britain and the United States. And as soon as they determined to conquer both of these great powers Japan left the League of Nations. Some years passed after that and the vast national resources were stored. We can't certify that since then we observed faithfully the international treaty which was very convenient only to Britain or U.S.A and unpreferable to the other countries. The national strength was intensified very much more.

156

3. When shall the present war end? That is when Britain and the United States shall surrender to Japan, or that Britain shall be wiped out of existence. Great effort and long years shall be necessary for us to destroy the British. The war has opened under expectation that the war should be continued for fifty years or a century or longer.

4. All preparation in order to destroy the British and United States were arranged very secretly with sufficient care. The strength of the nation was a secret from any country, even our own people did not know our strength and preparation, much less the foreigner. While German and French people propagated exaggeratedly about their Siegfried or Maginot line, Britain and United States propagated their superior power, over confidence of their strength with little regard to the training or their army. The Japanese made their very best effort to strengthen their power more and more.

There is a word among the Japanese Navy men 'Double Mondays and Fridays and no Sunday and Saturday a week' that means they have no holidays in a week. The training was so thorough, for example each pilot of the Japanese Air Force was completely trained so that he could be able to dash in funnel of the enemy's battleship with bombs loaded on the plane, thus causing instantly the sinking of the enemy's battleship at the sacrifice of his plane and life.

Nevertheless we overlooked the low estimate of the British and American side in comparison with our strength intentionally in order to throw them off their guard.

5. Thus at last war was declared on Britain and America and since the opening we have achieved many glorious victories. During the first half year Hong Kong, the base of the British Empire in the Far East fell, Singapore which was called the most impregnable fortress in the world fell, the Philippines Islands were captured from the United States and the Dutch and British East Indies Islands have also been occupied by the brave Japanese

157

soldiers. Overcoming French-Indo-China, going to alliance with Thai, now we are pressing all India. What of India? The committee of the all India national conference passed a resolution that all British must be withdrawn from India on the first of this month. In the Pacific from Aleutian island in the North to New Guinea in the South all the surface of the ocean including islands to New Guinea in the South all the surface of the ocean including islands in it are under control of our great fleet and Australia is under big bombing from our Air Force.

Just three or four days ago in the sea near Australia a British Great convoy fleet was attacked by our fleet. Twenty seven ships including thirteen battleships and cruisers were sunk and 68 aeroplanes were shot down by the Japanese force. The successful fight is moreover extending.

6. Thus the war situation is developing advantageously for Japan. We are now in the state to get freely petroleum, tin and rubber, food supplies are also plentiful. Now Great Japan controls all territories which supply all necessary materials for war and the ocean's surface on which the ships transports the materials.

The British and Unites States Navy combined who had the advantage of being able to conquer the Japanese Navy in the ratio of 10 to 3 were so badly destroyed and decreased in strength, that their proportion will never be able to dominate the Japanese fleet.

Thus the victory in the end is firmly on the head of Japan.

7. The Germany Army have taken Sevastopol, dominated over the black sea, occupying Rostov and dashing into the Caucasus. In Africa, German and Italian ally armies are very near to Cairo.

8. If the USSR had real power she could have attacked the back of Japan during her operations in the tropic zone, or she could also have made a counterattack to the Germans during the winter campaign, but the USSR could not do both and she is now

being routed and Germany has the store of corn and oil well districts. Inside Russia an anti-Starlin (sic) party is rapidly growing.

The defeat of the USSR as well as the submission of Britain and the United States, especially the fall of Britain is now the problem of time.

9. Thus we fought and now we are surprised to see the weakness of Britain and United States, which is more than we expected first and even feel compassion for them.

We thought at first that Anglo-Saxons are a self-asserted and un-relieveable race. But seeing many prisoners in the various frontiers we reconsidered that they might understand if we explain the purpose of our war and relative merits.

That is more compatible to the spirit of Hakko-wo Ie-to nasu to catch the enemy alive and amend their evil ways than to make all of them perish.

10. So we want now to teach our real intention to the British and American people and relieve them from an unhappy end. That is why we intend to propagate so as to rescue Britain and United States from their fate. Naturally Japan is not a country of propaganda and its propagandists have not got much experience, so she needs some co-operation with those who have good talent in this way. That is why we want to recommend you to the Japanese Radio Broadcasting Bureau. They will pay you a salary of Rs. 500 monthly to you if you are willing to assist them.

11. The Japanese have a different idea of war imprisonment from you. Your people seem to become war-prisoners shamelessly. And your Government also consider well of them as those who did their best. But the Japanese people think imprisonment the most disgraceful thing and prefer death. The interchange of prisoners cannot be applied to Japan. The rules as to the treatment of war-prisoners made under the restraint of the British or the United States (then the powers) should be changed according to the Japanese idea.

12. You threw down your arms and took an oath to give up all resistance, but we see some among you are not yet obedient to us in their mind and dare not co-operate with us. The war in the modern age is not decided only by the army power by total strength of the nation. In such an age it is necessary that the victory shall include the line of thoughts. Though you might think it enough to lay down your arms, we should never admit those who are not obedient even in their thoughts or spirit as a true surrender. We are mindful to dispose of such fellows as we like irrespective of life or the war-prisoner rules.

Our country is requiring of every man his best efforts in his own position in the slogan of 'Develop Power,' much more she requires from every prisoner naturally his full efforts by mental or labour work.

It is arranged that almost all of you, irrespectively of being under our inspection or not, shall be engaged in constructing works of road under supervision of our soldiers.

13. Probably you used to think that the propaganda by your enemies was always advantageous to them and did harm to your country. But Japanese propaganda is a different case. You should recognise that this will rescue your country at the end from destruction.

Besides you may be afraid of any trouble that may be caused when you return home if you assist in Japanese propagation. But such fear is unnecessary, because your name and rank will be profoundly taken care of and will not be exposed and also the Japanese terms of peace shall include a term that the enemy country shall not be able to trouble in any way those who co-operated with Japan but will protect them. We shall never admit any peace if the above term is not absolutely agreed upon. We hold a firm conviction in victory.

14. So if Britain or United States are not able to comprehend the Japanese true intention and consequently remain

to fight, their way is only to their grave. Moreover you should know that you may be unable to live to reach your country.

We are calling for volunteers who are willing to co-operate in this holy propaganda act of Japan so that you shall be able to rescue your nation from the ruin, quicken your chance of returning home and surely enjoy the far more comfortable life during the war in the cherry-blossoming country.

If you wish to volunteer write 'yes' and your signature, rank and prison number, if not write 'no' and the same.

APPENDIX B

EXTRACT FROM BRUCE TOOTHILL'S DIARY

LIST OF BOOKS WORTH READING ACQUIRED
OUTSIDE AND READ WHILE IN GAOL (1942-45)

	TITLE	AUTHOR
1.	Blank on the Map	Eric Shipton
2.	The Old Curiosity Shop	Dickens
3.	Hard Times	Dickens
4.	David Copperfield	Dickens
5.	The Rabbit King of Russia	Ureh
6.	Jew Suss	Feuchtwanger
7.	July, 1914	Emil Ludwig
8.	As We Were	E.F. Benson
9.	Salute to Adventure	Buchan
10.	English Journey	Priestley
11.	In Chancery (Forsyte Saga)	Galsworthy
12.	Waltzing Matilda	Haskell
13.	Out of this Nettle	Norah Lofts
14.	Should the War Spread	DN Pritt, KC
15.	Frenchman's Creek	Daphne du Maurier
16.	The Defenders	Hoellering (Austrian)
17.	Ah, King	Somerset Maughan
18.	Burma and Beyond	Sir George Scott
19.	The House of Marku	Unnto Sefassem (Finnish)
20.	Landfall	Neville Shute
21.	Crime and Punishment	Dostoevsky
22.	Peter Jackson	Gilbert Frankau
23.	Voltaire	Andre Maurois

24.	Wuthering Heights	Emily Bronte
25.	Napoleon	H.A.L. Fisher
26.	Sylvia Scarlett	Compton Mackenzie
27.	The Brothers	L.A.G. Strong
28.	Harvest of the North	J.L. Hobson
29.	Robinson Crusoe	Defoe
30.	Mansfield Park	Jane Austen
31.	Germinal	Emil Zola
32.	Eminent Victorians (4)	Lytton Strachey
33.	In Search of Ireland	H.V. Morton
34.	A Kind of Insolence	Margaret Stein
35.	Massini	Bolton King
36.	Outline of History	H.G. Wells
37.	The Story of Philosophy	Durrant
38.	Spanish House	Eleanor Smith
39.	1000 Beautiful Things. Verse, Prose and Pictures	Selected by Arthur Mee
40.	The Big Fellow (Michael Collins)	O'Connor
41.	Our Mutual Friend	Dickens
42.	Dombey & Son	Dickens
43.	The Uncommercial Traveller	Dickens
44.	The Fair Maid of Perth	Walter Scott

Not one of the above was issued by the Japanese. They were all brought in against orders, besides some 150 others not worth recording. Over and above this the men managed to scrounge Bibles, Text Books, Dictionaries and even a Pitman's Shorthand Vocabulary.

Without the aid of such things I don't know how we should have managed to kill time for the three year period.'

APPENDIX C

Headquarters
CONFIDENTIAL
HQ Jullunder Area
5 Sept 1945

Subject: Treatment of POWs in Japanese Hands

1.   Although the following facts were given verbally to the interrogating officers by recovered POWs from Rangoon early in May this year, I wish to place them on record again to ensure that the ends of justice are met.

2.   Captain MITSUNORI KOSHIMA was the first Japanese Commandant of the Field Prison Camp in Rangoon, a position which he held until 15 September 1942, when he was relieved by a Lieutenant SAKIMOTA.

During that period he was personally guilty of various acts of brutality against officers and must also be held responsible for a number of unprovoked assaults by members of his staff.

3.   His most heinous crime was the virtual murder of Captain H.M. KILGOUR, RAMC, who, having contracted dysentery while in solitary Confinement was allowed neither medicines nor medical attention of any sort, and was only moved to the hospital ward for British POWs the day before he died, when he was already unconscious and moribund.

4.   In his attempt to persuade British officers to broadcast, he employed starvation and beatings in certain cases and finally organised what came to be known as "the blood bath"* of August

164

17th 1942, where all those officers were paraded to be beaten by Burman POWs in the presence of Indian POWs.

5.   He was particularly brutal to the late Brigadier C.D. Hobson, who in the course of two months, when in solitary Confinement, was starved for varying period amounting to 21 days in all, and was severely beaten on at least one occasion.

6.   Captain KOSHIMA was promoted major on leaving the Prison Camp, and was seen in Rangoon shortly afterwards by POW working parties. He was reported to have left Rangoon about the end of September 1942, and sometime later there was a report in one of the Japanese newspapers of a Major KOSHIMA having been killed on one of the islands of, I think, the New Guinea Archipelago.

Whether this was the same man was never substantiated but I think it unlikely that he could have survived the war. He was typical of the fanatical type of Japanese Regular Army officer and if he had not been killed in action, will in all probability have saved his face in the traditional manner.

SIGNED   H.R. POWER
Colonel

* NOTE: I discovered this letter in a file of documents lodged at the Imperial War Museum by Captain R A Willy Wilding when I was researching on 30 December 1997. I was surprised at Colonel Power's reference to the 'blood bath.' I never heard him refer to it as such; but it is true that others did. Probably he did not want to go into the episode in any detail and needed to describe it somehow. But if anyone was entitled to describe the 'Broadcasting Parade' as a 'Blood bath' that person was Colonel Power.

C.R.L.C.

APPENDIX D

FULL CIRCLE

In his book *Defeat into Victory* Field Marshall Slim records that at the end of July 1944 'the 17th Indian Division was on its way to a well-earned rest. It had been actively engaged since December 1941. That is for two years and eight months, and almost all that time in direct contact with the enemy. A record I should think.' By mid-February 1945 it was back in action again advancing to and capturing Meiktila.

During the whole of that time, 7 Baluch, reconstituted after its near annihilation at the Battle of Pa-an, was part of the Division. When the Japanese surrendered in August 1945, the battalion was in the front line of the Sittang River, about 50 miles from where it had started in January 1942. The only two officers still with the Battalion, who had been in the Battle of Pa-an, were John Randle and Siri Kanth Korla. Both at that time were Majors. In November 1945 they were both invited to a guest night by a Battalion of Gurkhas in their Brigade. This battalion was located in Pa-an, which also contained a large number of Japanese prisoners of war.

On the way to Pa-an they visited the scene of the battle. In the final chapter, entitled 'Full Circle' of his book of wartime reminiscences, (written for private circulation) John Randle has described this visit and an extraordinary episode that evening at the Gurkhas' guest night in Pa-an.

The chapter was indeed well-named. It gives me considerable satisfaction that two of the 7 Baluch officers, both of whom fought with distinction in the Battle of Pan-an, survived the next three and a half years to experience this total reversal of fortune. John Randle kindly gave me permission to refer to this episode.

166

But I found it impossible to paraphrase his description without losing both its dramatic effect and what are to me its evocative references to the battlefield. With his agreement, I now quote the last part of his chapter *Full Circle* which has subsequently been included in an anthology of personal experiences of the Burma Campaign entitled *Tales from the Burma Campaign 1942-1945*. I make no comment except to state that it is nice to have some well-written paragraphs in my Memories.

'Siri and I wandered over the scene of the battalion battle, but four monsoons and four years of tropical growth had made much of it unrecognisable. It was a melancholy business.

'We crossed over the Salween to a very cordial welcome from the Gurkhas, who had established their mess most comfortably in the township. Siri and I were of course staying the night and when we entered the Mess before dinner, their Colonel welcomed us warmly and said "We know what you two chaps and your battalion suffered here nearly four years ago. You should know that out in the rain (there was an unseasonal deluge outside) standing rigidly to attention, are a thousand Japanese. They will stand there until you give the order for their dismissal. And what would you like to drink?" I have to admit (and comparing notes with Siri afterwards he felt the same) a slight feeling of embarrassment. Clearly the Gurkhas intended this as a special compliment to us - almost an exorcism of the ghosts of defeat and death which the place represented to us - and it would have been churlish not to have responded in the spirit in which it was offered. The Gurkhas were ever hard men.

'After several drinks and just before we went into dinner, we suggested to our hosts that perhaps they might wish to dismiss the Japanese, and this they did. I heard later that the reason for this penance had been explained to the Japanese, that they accepted it as entirely right and proper, and that every man-jack of them stood there in the rain, unwaveringly at attention, like Guardsmen on Horse Guards Parade, for the whole thirty or forty minutes. One could not but admire them.

'Siri and I drove away from that haunted place the next morning with mild hangovers, but with a great lightness of spirit. The war was finally over.'

APPENDIX E

BURMA REVISITED
28th January to 3rd February 1976
(Edited Extract from original paper)

On the 28th January 1976, June and I landed at Mingaladon Airport, Rangoon in a party of 23 visiting Burma, Bangkok, Bali and Java, organised by Serenissima Travel - a small travel agency - which at that time specialised in visiting places containing art treasures and antiquities.

When in Rangoon we stayed at the new Russian-built hotel on the Inya Lake in beautiful surroundings.

I had been told by Bruce Toothill, who visited Burma a year ago, that he had not found it possible to visit the jail. He suggested that my best chance might be to 'chat up' the Burmese girl, who would be in charge of our travel arrangements, and try to persuade her to obtain the necessary permission. I did so. She gave me this information. A road now ran through the old jail. The prisoners, who had occupied it until a year or so ago, had been removed elsewhere. What was left of the jail was used as a military barracks for the training of young soldiers.

In the late afternoon of our second day following our return from Pegu, to which I will refer later, June and I with three others, hired a taxi to take us from the Inya Lake Hotel for a pre-dinner 'sundowner' at the Strand Hotel ('Colonial Baroque' in the now decaying commercial district by the Rangoon River). At our request he drove into Rangoon down the Prome Road which now goes 'slap through' the old jail. It is a dual carriageway. On the left there are a number of small stores, reputedly the centre of the black-market in Rangoon. One can see from the remains of the old jail wall that the whole of this is within the confines of the old jail. All the buildings on the left side of the road have been destroyed. On the right of the road are the prison blocks and central water tower. Four or five Burmese soldiers were standing guard on the right of the entrance holding their rifles in both hands and with fixed bayonets. It was a curious and exciting experience to see these buildings with the well-remembered steps down from the first floor, after so many years. I walked straight through the new entrance followed by June and the others, half expecting to be pursued by a shout of "KURA! ATSUMARE!" ("You there. Come here.") With their green uniforms and inscrutable oriental faces, the Burmese soldiers were not unlike the Japanese guards. I stopped by the water tower and was joined by the others as I was finding it difficult to find my bearings and to identify each particular Block. Uncertainty had taken the place of our confident march into the jail and produced the result one would have expected. It was made quite clear that we were not allowed there and had to leave at once, back past the immobile but watching Burmese guards.

I then continued down the Prome Road, turned right and a little further on walked into the old entrance to the jail. The corridor of the Old Japanese guardhouse was longer than I remembered. It is occupied by numerous Burmese families and there were chickens running around in what used to be the Japanese guard room. The end of the corridor into the prison was boarded up but I was able to see through into the jail and this time I found my bearings. Unfortunately, my time was short and I had to return to the others who were waiting with the taxi at the corner of the Prome Road surrounded by friendly, laughing Burmese children.

On the morning after our arrival, we had driven to Pegu (to look at the Shwemawday Pagoda and the grotesque reclining Gautama Buddha). The distance is 55 miles and made me realise how tough it was for those of us who were marched out by the Japanese at the end of April 1945 after so many years of captivity.

I also noticed how little real cover from aerial view there was on either side of the road.

I identified the sparsely-wooded, grassy glade on the left of the road where we stopped for our meal on the first evening. I was able to narrow down to a choice of two, the small wood about 100 yards off the road on the right where we had our first long halt. As we were nearing Pegu I was watching the terrain on the left of the road to locate the place where we lay up for the whole day in the bamboo thickets above a line of a few empty Burmese houses along the road and were subjected to such continuous air activity. Suddenly there was an explosion, as the right front tyre of our coach burst beneath where I was sitting. We must have been travelling at about 50 m.p.h. and skidded for over 50 yards. The driver just - but only just - managed to keep the coach from going over the bank into the rice field on the right. We finally stopped 2 ft. in front of a tree and with perhaps 10 yards of tyre marks along the non-metalled part of the road within 6 inches of the bank. This was sufficiently deep and steep to have been certain to overturn the vehicle which being old and hot would probably have caught fire. It was generally agreed that anyone who escaped serious injury would have been extremely lucky. There were some Burmese houses along the opposite side of the road with paths and a sunken road passing through bamboo thickets behind. I wandered through these while the wheel was being changed. A study of the terrain on our way back from Pegu confirmed my very strong original impression that this was where we had spent that day with our planes zooming overhead and machine gunning the road below us. I remember it as one of the least pleasant of my life. It was ironical that I came nearer to death only a few yards away in peaceful conditions some 30 years later.

APPENDIX F

Speech on the occasion of the Dinner attended by the former
officers of the 7th/10th Baluch Regiment and their wives
and
presided over by Brigadier J.P. Randle OBE, MC
at
the Army & Navy Club on the 12th February 1992
to mark the 50th Anniversary of the Battle of Pa-an

Ladies and Gentlemen

I feel very honoured to be asked to speak at this dinner when we are commemorating not only the 50th Anniversary of the Battle of Pa-an but also the very fine achievements of 7 Baluch over the subsequent three years of warfare against the Japanese, in which I was the only one of the Baluchi Officers present to play no part.

I would like to thank you John for the most generous terms in which you have introduced me.

John Randle, Bill Greenwood and I are the only survivors of the Battle present tonight. Sadly Pat Dunn, George Holden and Hugh Mercer are no longer with us.

In his letter last May suggesting this dinner, John wrote that the Battle of Pa-an was arguably the most famous Battle fought by 7 Baluch but it was the least successful in terms of military success. I agree with him. The Battle of Pa-an was a comprehensive defeat. To pretend otherwise would in my view diminish the remarkable achievements of Pat Lindsay and those Officers who served with and after him in rebuilding 7 Baluch into what became as John has said one of the finest Battalions in Burma, playing a significant part in several victories over the Japanese.

Despite the defeat of 7 Baluch at Pa-an by what was unarguably a better trained, vastly more experienced, formidable Japanese force with complete air superiority, which they had exploited in low-level bombing attacks on our position in previous days, there are I believe many reasons why it is appropriate to commemorate the 50th Anniversary of the Battle of Pa-an.

Foremost of all is the fact that in the Battle in the early hours of the morning of 12th February 1942 - 50 years ago today - some 550 Officers, VCO's and Men of 7 Baluch were killed or became prisoners of war of the Japanese. There were many more killed than taken prisoner, and of these many did not survive the War.

I will not attempt to describe the Battle. Because it mainly took place in darkness, because of the nature of the terrain with its areas of thick jungle and because we were overrun by the Japanese in the end, I have really never known all that took place. But I do want to mention some fine performances which, either from my own observation or from talking to survivors, I know are true.

The brunt of the Japanese Attack when it came at about 1.00 a.m. fell up Siri's C Company of Dogras, who put up a magnificent fight. As most of you know Siri[18] was awarded the DSO for his conduct during the Battle. John did circulate copies of a letter from Siri from India in which he wrote how 'very very happy and much thrilled' he was to receive the invitation to this dinner and conveyed his 'heartiest congratulations and good wishes' to all Officers attending.

The Japs also attacked B Company commanded by John Randle with Bill Greenwood as his Company Officer. B Company had been depleted by the loss of two platoons - one annihilated by the Japs the night before to the south where the Japs had crossed the river Salween in force and the other out on patrol. They stood their ground and put up a fine fighting performance until they were overrun.

173

One of the survivors of the Battle is Toots - Captain Bruce Toothill, the Quartermaster, now 84 years of age and unable to travel from the Isle of Man because of his old leg wound. After the Battle was over, he and Subedar-Major Kirpa Ram - a splendid formidable soldier - with a small party were trying to reach the road to Duyinzeik when they ran into some Japs. In the ensuing engagement the Subedar-Major - a powerful man - was killed grappling with a Jap and Toots was severely wounded. I believe that he was the only one of our wounded taken prisoner by the Japs at Pa-an. With next to no medical attention it is remarkable that he is alive today.

Lastly, I would like to pay tribute to the CO Lt. Colonel Jerry Dyer who was killed at Pa-an. I personally witnessed his exceptional courage and his total indifference to enemy fire.

There were I am sure many other brave performances in the jungle which went unwitnessed by any survivor. But I hope that I have said enough to show how right we are to mark the 50th Anniversary of the Battle of Pa-an and to remember the many comrades and friends who died there.

NOBUKO KOSUGE PAYS HER TRIBUTE AT THE CAMBRIDGE REMEMBRANCE SERVICE. NOVEMBER 1996.

APPENDIX G

Episode At The War Memorial In The Cemetery at Cambridge On Remembrance Day 1996

On the 11th November 1996 the Cambridge Evening News carried a colour photograph filling much of the front page of Mrs Nobuko Kosuge, dressed in kimono and obi, kneeling in front of the war memorial at the cemetery. Mrs Kosuge was the wife of one of the Japanese research students working in Cambridge University and was herself quite an authority on wartime problems, having translated a book on the Tokyo war crimes trials, and written a book on her own. This is the accompanying story:

A former prisoner of war in the Far East broke down in tears when a Japanese woman fell on her knees to beg forgiveness for her country at the Cambridge Remembrance ceremony.

The highly charged moment came during a weekend of ceremonies in Mid-Anglia to honour the war dead.

Nobuko Kosuge, a visiting scholar at Wolfson College, asked to attend the ceremony when Poppy collector Jack Hunter called at her Clarkson Road home.

She was invited to the ceremony at the City Cemetery attended by representatives of the services, including holders of the Burma Star.

Mr Hunter, 75, of Oxford Road, said she was shaking like a leaf all day. One prisoner of war went up to her and said he had vowed never to speak to a Japanese person until then.

We had to prise them away from each other. They were both in tears. She later attended a ceremony at Cherry Hinton and

175

was told by another ex-prisoner of war that she had been very brave.

Vic Taylor of Teversham, Vice-President of the local Burma Star Association said: "One member said that after seeing her lay a wreath it had changed his mind about speaking to the Japanese." It was rather moving.

Ron Wells, branch secretary of the Cherry Hinton Branch of the British Legion said: "This could be the beginning of a bridge being built between the two nations."

FOOTNOTES

[1]Subsequently Sir John Smyth M.P. and government minister in the fifties.

[2]7 Baluch consisted of two Companies of PMs (B&D). One Company of Pathans (A) and one Company of Dogras (C). Our Dogras were Dogra Brahmins and different from the Dogra Rajputs in the 17th Dogra Regiment. The platoons in HQ Company were mixed.

[3]The quoted extracts from this book have been made with the express permission of Ian Lyall Grant.

[4]On the 9th June 1995 I met David Penn, an expert on pistols, in the armoury of the Imperial War Museum. After I had shown him how the Jap had grabbed my pistol just before I pulled the trigger, he explained and demonstrated to me how this action could have affected the mechanism and caused a misfire, despite the fact that the pistol was fully loaded and the cylinder rotated when I pulled the trigger. In his opinion this was almost certainly the cause of the misfire which had always puzzled me, but which certainly saved my life.

[5]'Tamasha' Urdu for 'show.'

[6]Urdu for 'seize.'

[7]In my opinion Toots was guilty of an uncharacteristic exaggeration when he made this remark - but perhaps I was unaware of what I was eating!

[8]The forty or so of us in the two officers' barrack rooms had a

separate cookhouse from the BORs.

[9]My authority for this paragraph is *The Railway Man* by Eric Lomax (published by Jonathan Cape 1995).

[10]I have in my possession an account by retired Subedar (in 1942 Jemadar) Charam Dass of this escape and of how he succeeded in rejoining 7 Baluch at Meiktila in February 1943.

[11]I am indebted to Bill Gover for reminding me of this anecdote.

[12]It has been pointed out to me that this was a misquotation on my part. With the assistance of my eldest grand-daughter at Bristol University I have learnt that the correct quotation should have been: 'Abandon hope all ye who enter here' from Dante's *Inferno*.

[13]I attended Philip Stibbe's memorial service at Norwich Cathedral on 25th April 1997. It has a capacity for about 1000 and was full. He had been headmaster of Norwich School from 1975 until his retirement in 1984 due to ill health. There was also a separate memorial service at Bradfield College where he had been a housemaster for 21 years. There was a three column obituary and photograph in The Times.

[14]In fact at the time I had no intention of ever writing my memoirs!

[15]I was promoted under the new regulations from Second Lieutenant to Lieutenant on 1st October 1942.

[16]The other two officers from 7 Baluch, Bruce Toothill (still suffering from his wounds) and Jake Jervis, were among the sick left in Rangoon. The Japs departed on 29 April. After several anxious days they were rescued by our troops landing from the sea.

[17]This is a charity, established and funded by the Sasakawa Company one of Japan's industrial giants, with the object of promoting a new understanding between Great Britain and Japan to replace the bitterness of the war years.

[18]Captain Siri Kanth Korla - later Major-General Korla DSO MC Indian Army.

ACKNOWLEDGEMENTS

I am most grateful to so many who have given a reluctant author, such as I am, the help and encouragement without which I could not have told my story.

The staff of the Imperial War Museum were consistently helpful to me in my researches. All photographs in this book, with the exception of those containing a picture of me, came from the Museum's Photographic Archive and I am grateful for being given permission to reproduce them.

I am particularly grateful to Mrs Eleanor Holland for giving me permission to quote from the unpublished diary and writings of her father, the late Colonel Henry Power, to Mrs Joy Stibbe for giving me permission to quote from the book written by her late husband, Philip Stibbe, entitled *Return via Rangoon* published by Leo Cooper in 1994 and to Major-General Ian Lyall Grant for giving me permission to quote from the book entitled *Burma 1942 The Japanese Invasion,* published in 1999 by the Zampi Press of Chichester.

My wife June, my daughter Pauline, my son David and my eldest grand-daughter Eleanor have been most supportive.

I am greatly indebted to a number of friends who in one way or another have helped and encouraged me.

I am particularly grateful to Brigadier John Randle for his general encouragement, his professional opinion on the events before, during and after the Battle of Pa-an and his permission to quote from his unpublished writings, to the late Bruce Toothill for giving me permission to quote from his diaries and to Bill Gover for making available to me some of his unpublished writings and assisting me on several points of detail.

I am also most grateful to the following who have either helped or encouraged me or both, namely: Tom Adams, Malcolm Bradbury, the late John Butler, Philippa Butler, Jim Connell, Subedar

Charam Dass, Tom Davis, John Fuller, Dick Graveson, Dennis Hill, Dennis Johnson, Michael Kerr, Judy and Tom Kneale, Margaret Polhill, Tony Rieck and my brother-in-law Philip Seymour.

I am also indebted to Frances Charlesworth who has brilliantly transcribed my indistinct dictation and my publishers Richard and Diana Holderness for the infinite trouble they have taken.